# CHALLENGE AND RESPONSE
### A programme for Europe

# Franz Josef Strauss

# *CHALLENGE AND RESPONSE*
## *A programme for Europe*

With a foreword by
JEAN-JACQUES SERVAN-SCHREIBER

translated by HENRY FOX

Weidenfeld and Nicolson
5 Winsley Street London W1

Originally published in Germany under the title:
*Herausforderung und Antwort: Ein Programm
für Europa* by Seewald Verlag, Stuttgart

©Seewald Verlag Dr. Heinrich Seewald,
Stuttgart-Degerloch 1968

English translation © by Weidenfeld and Nicolson Ltd

First published in Great Britain 1969

SBN 297 17950 0

Printed by Cox & Wyman Ltd., London, Reading and
Fakenham

# Contents

## PUBLISHER'S NOTE

The resignation of President de Gaulle in April 1969 has necessitated slight amendments to the original text of this book.

# *Foreword*

The procedure that has been adopted here is unusual: a Minister of the German Federal Republic currently in office, one of his country's most prominent politicians, has asked a Frenchman to write the foreword for a book to be published in the Minister's own country. It is all the more unusual as the German problem is the central theme of the book. A non-German cannot possibly deal with such matters with the same degree of sympathetic understanding, nor can he be expected to bring as much expertise to bear on the subject as Herr Strauss.

No doubt, Herr Strauss was anxious for a Frenchman to confirm that the German problem concerns the whole of Europe. No one will contradict him. No Frenchman, no European can remain indifferent in the face of the fact that other Europeans are being denied the right of self-determination; faced with such a denial a German might conceive the idea, engendered by nationalism, that Germany's reunification is a matter that concerns him alone. Herr Strauss says to his fellow-countrymen: If you approach the problem of reunification exclusively from the standpoint of the nation State, you are bound to scare your neighbours, for a re-unified Germany would undoubtedly be the greatest European Power west of Russia. And he says to the other Europeans: If you wish to avoid the emergence of such an excessively large Germany, you must ensure that the latter becomes an integral part of a united Europe.

No European must close his mind to the fact that there is an historic opportunity within our grasp to establish a community which would meet the needs of the modern world. It is up to all of us to ensure that our sons – may they be Piedmontese, Bavarians or Burgundians – do not reproach us one day with having bequeathed to them a world in which they have no say and where they play no part in the race for progress. It is one of the greatest merits of Herr Strauss's book that he deals frankly with the crux of the problem. The entire book is inspired by the conviction that man does not live by bread – or his car – alone. André Malraux once said that it was man's ambition to ensure that his actions 'leave a mark upon the earth'. This is why Herr Strauss replies to the question whether Europe should be a Power, without hypocrisy and without evasion, with an unambiguous 'yes'. There are two different realities behind this 'yes'. With one of them I am familiar, having tried to deal with it in my book *The American Challenge*. The problem for Europe is to be second to none in technology, science and culture both today and in the future. The other reality belongs to the classical realm of politics. The problem here is to devise ways of persuading the Soviet Union to discuss Europe's future with the Europeans themselves instead of confining itself to a dialogue with the other Super-Power, the USA. In this connection, Herr Strauss is thinking of a united Western Europe which would sooner or later have at its disposal all the attributes of power, including nuclear power.

Such a vision implies profound doubts about the status quo. Naturally, it entails dangers of its own. It is our task to weigh these dangers against those which would follow from the maintenance of the status quo. The present situation in Europe is determined by two characteristic features: the East's failure to achieve anything like a genuine integration, and the West's failure to create a real federation.

Ever since his youth, Stalin was preoccupied with the nationality problem in the Soviet Union. In January 1918 he published the 'Proclamation of the Rights of the Peoples of Russia'. He had two tactical objectives in mind: The national ideal and regional languages were to be resuscitated everywhere; at the same time, however, a single all-powerful party was to guarantee that all political and economic affairs were subject to undisputed central-ized control. This policy was pursued with the utmost ruthlessness. In order to make everyone feel that he was enjoying cultural independence, steps were even taken to introduce the use of languages and dialects which had heretofore hardly been known to exist. On the other hand, the chairman of every local soviet had a Party secretary sitting by his side – and these officials were mostly of Russian background – who wielded real power. Terror, propaganda, but, let us admit, also the fact that the population is genuinely interested in sharing in the economic progress of the Soviet Union – as well as a system of education which offers real equality of opportunity – have enabled this system to survive to this day.

However, when it came to be applied to Eastern Europe the system failed lamentably. While allowing a sham folklore nationalism to exist there, the Kremlin took good care to install a leadership in each of the Communist Parties which could be relied on to dance to its tune. In this way, the armies, the administrations and the economies of Eastern Europe were colonized. No doubt, the absence of a generous policy did much to wreck the Soviet Union's hopes. Instead of being allowed to share in the progress of the entire area, the countries of Eastern Europe were made to contribute a great deal more to the development of the Soviet Union – by means of war reparations and as a result of the inequitable currency rates enforced – than the Soviet Union ever contributed to them. Moreover, the absence of convertible currencies slowed down trade between the East European countries to such an extent that they could not but feel humiliated by their utter dependence on the Soviet Union which resulted from this state of affairs. It was not very long before the peoples of these countries, whose national awareness is, when all is said and done, somewhat more developed than that of, say, the Turkmenians, came to regard this situation as unacceptable, the more so as, unlike the Turkmenians, they are exposed to the impact of broadcasting; all they have to do is to switch on their set to find out that right on their doorstep, in Western Europe, abundance and liberty are to be found existing side by side.

It is because of this that the 'Prague Spring' occurred in 1968 and that we witnessed the emergence of Czechoslovakia's 'socialism in one country'. Such a 'socialism in one country' is, however, bound to lead to varying developments in individual countries. What amounted to democracy in Czechoslovakia for a brief spell now threatens to become nationalism pure and simple, and even xenophobia and antisemitism, in Poland. As for Eastern Germany, it may one day achieve a Prussian form of socialism and a new leadership there might become tempted to enter into an exclusive dialogue with the people on the other bank of the river Elbe, with whom they share a common language. If this were to happen, the system established by the Soviets would finally collapse and the USSR might be driven to further acts of the kind of violence of which the invasion of Czechoslovakia in 1968 gave us a bitter foretaste.

At the same time, the West's efforts to set up a federation have also failed, in spite of the fact that the Americans – resisting the temptation to engage in the time-honoured pursuit of *divide et impera* – put their faith in this great ideal when they launched the Marshall Plan. However, the weight of history has proved too great. In the eyes of many Germans, the Europe which was to be built was merely a welcome means of purging themselves of the sins of Nazism, while many Frenchmen, accustomed to the presence of a centralized State since Louis XIV, failed to see how valuable the concept of a supranational structure could be to the various peoples in helping them not only to conserve but to enhance their own heritage. As for the Americans, who were left after the war shouldering the greatest responsibilities, they have been apt to confuse the concepts of 'leadership', 'community' and 'partnership'. These misunderstandings reached their culmination in 1954 with the failure of the plans for a European Defence Community. Too many Germans saw in this scheme nothing but a means of achieving their own rehabilitation; too many Frenchmen saw in it only a certain loss of sovereignty, and too many Americans regarded it as no more than a convenient instrument. The fact that the EEC had been a success has not in itself changed this situation to any extent. True, the practice of free trade has proved useful in combating the old protectionist habits of the past, but the EEC is not strong enough to set in motion an industrial policy holding genuine promise for the future.

A hosiery mill can exist perfectly well within a national market; on the other hand, for the electronics and aircraft industries the EEC is hardly large enough. Here State intervention is needed. Herr Strauss is quite right in pointing out that two thirds of the twenty thousand million dollars which the USA spends annually on research comes from State subsidies. However, we have no

'United States of Western Europe'. Thanks to the lack of a common taxation system and budgeting, thanks to the lack of a common policy, Western Europe has to contend with duplication and waste. As a result, her enterprises are faced with the choice between two alternatives: either they must allow themselves to become dependent on stronger American firms, or they must indulge in costly national adventures on the lines of the French 'Plan Calcul'. In short, the danger is clear. Western Germany has essentially remained the national Germany of the past while Eastern Germany may yet go the same way, so much so that one day we may witness a reunification of the German people accomplished along lines not foreseen in the book of rules laid down by the peoples of Europe, above all by Russia and France. If this were to happen, we should be face to face with precisely that explosive situation which Chancellor Adenauer feared and warned against all his life.

What, then, are the dangers inherent in Herr Strauss's proposal, which is that a united Europe be created which would be sufficiently powerful to *compel* the Soviet Union to rethink the problems of Europe in their entirety? In theory, there are two such dangers: Europe's isolation within the Western orbit and the possibility that the Soviet Union might be forced back into a sort of ghetto.

No one knows better than Herr Strauss that a genuine solution of our international monetary problems calls for concerted action by a united Europe and the United States. He realizes, too, that a solution to the agrarian problems of the world, especially that of mass hunger, as well as the provision of effective assistance to the developing countries, also require such action. It must be admitted, however, that the United States, too, suffers from certain super-power reflexes, and its co-operation in such schemes would strike an even more artificial note if it were to indulge in the notion that the only conceivable purpose of a unified Europe is to serve as an instrument of military power.

Although Herr Strauss refuses to contemplate a nuclear war or even to regard it as thinkable, and although, moreover, he excludes any recourse to threats or blackmail, he nevertheless insists that any negotiations with the Soviet Union must be conducted from a position of strength – not only economic but also military strength. The least one can say of this notion is that its application would introduce a new element into world politics and that this new element could be dangerous. None the less 'we ought not to allow ourselves to become paralysed by this fear if such an approach really does provide the key to a successful policy. We should be ill-advised, however, if we were to take the Soviet Union's cries of alarm too lightly. Whether we like it or not, the USSR cannot forget the loss of twenty million men and women in the last war. Moreover, despite its gigantic armoury, this colossus remains notably vulnerable both in the economic and social fields. The explosion which occurred in France in May 1968 and its well-known sequels are as nothing compared with what could happen in the Soviet Union one day. Here is a country which, though it gives all its children access to modern education, at the same time bars its youth from free thought and a free life. Here, too, is a country where brilliant technological achievements seem to go hand in hand with striking economic failures – where there are sputniks and, at the same time, a shortage of frying pans. How can one fail to see that the situation in such a country as this is bound to be fraught with vast dangers due to the accumulation of unsatisfied demands, some of which date back to the last century and others which are yet bound to arise in the century to come? How can one assume that such a country would feel sufficiently secure in its own strength to accept without a countervailing concession the collapse of the world system which it considers to be the guarantee of its security? What we should offer the Soviet Union is not a nuclear threat – not even a veiled one – but a colossal Marshall Plan, which a united Europe should offer it in the foreseeable future.

The fact is that the real contest between Europe and the United States is not at present taking place in the sphere of atomic armament. Its outcome will be decided by which of the two will be able to supply effective industrial aid to Russia when the time comes. A Europe which, though organized in the military sense, is inferior to America in economic terms would be bound to lose this genuine opportunity of achieving a negotiated solution of Europe's problems.

The failure of the European Defence Community in 1954 should be a lesson to us. In our day and age, a European authority with its finger on the atomic trigger is nothing but a mirage! The Germans, as Herr Strauss rightly points out, reject any attempt to discriminate against Man. It will be many years before a President of a United Europe is elected by popular ballot, and before this happens serious negotiations between Europe and the Soviet Union will long since have become necessary in view of the disintegration of Eastern Europe. In such a situation, what we need is that minimum abrogation of political sovereignty which will enable an effective economic – i.e. a political but not yet a military – organization to be established of the kind which is needed by Western Europe.

Do not let us lose sight of the fact that, together, the countries of Western Europe now have at their disposal larger reserves of gold and currency than did the USA at the end of the second world war. However, these reserves are to all intents and purposes frozen because they cannot be amalgamated. The experience through which France is going at the present time shows that any one of our countries is economically vulnerable, and thus politically powerless, so long as it remains on its own. It is the task of our generation to act resolutely in order to put an end to this state of affairs. A united Europe can, by virtue of its industrial strength and free political institutions, and without having recourse to military threats, become a focal point of attraction to the East. This is the new law which governs the great historic confrontations of our time: their imagination is capable of inspiring the peoples and of changing the map of the world, while nuclear weapons remain powerless since they cancel each other out.

We owe a debt of gratitude to Herr Strauss for having made us open the dialogue and think about these crucial problems without allowing ourselves to be blinkered by nationalist prejudices.

Jean-Jacques Servan-Schreiber

# *The Rise and Decline of Europe*

It is the custom in Germany more than in any other country to call for the political unity of Europe and to pledge one's best efforts on behalf of that unity. No politician, and in fact no public speaker of any standing – whatever his affiliation and no matter what the occasion on which he might be speaking – can afford not to at least pay lip service to this ideal, the more so as the European tide seems to be on the ascendant at the moment. Ever since the 'Atlantic wave' – the enthusiasm for the real or supposed possibilities of a drawing together of the continents on either side of the Atlantic – has begun to wane, not least because of the cool attitude of the Americans themselves towards this idea, we appear to be witnessing a resurgence of the 'European ideal'. 'Europe' has once again become all the rage in political fashion, among those at least who are not yet ready to accept a comfortable seat in a political grandstand, provided by courtesy of the USA, from which to watch events in the world arena as detached onlookers ready to accept whatever fate an uncertain future might have in store for them. But are we really witnessing a renaissance of the European ideal over wide areas of our continent ? Is it not rather a European 'resignation' that is occurring ? No one, it would seem, knows of a universally acceptable solution to the problem of Europe's political unity. No one knows of a path that would lead to a common future of the citizens, peoples and States of our part of the world. Is it the case, then, that Europe, for all the fine words that have been spoken about its unity as an ultimate goal, belongs to the past, to history, and is but an object of proud but rueful memory ? Is Europe really something more than a loose association of nations based on a common culture and civilization, is it really more than a convenient designation used in geography lessons to describe the Western promontory of Greater Asia which has been granted an enhanced status in recognition of its past services, is it really more than a rhetorical formula, a ritual incantation intended to conciliate the gods of history and to keep at bay the shadows of the future?

Up to the beginning of this century there was no need for Europe to be united since the position it occupied in civilization was unique. In fact, Europe did not consider itself a part of the world but regarded itself as 'the' world, no less. Born of the civilization of the Mediterranean and an amalgam of the Greek spirit, the Roman art of government and the Christian religion, it was later glorified in the achievements of the Latin, Teuton and Slav peoples, which both absorbed this civilization and developed it further. In this way, Europe shaped the world and had every right to consider herself its focal point; not its dead centre perhaps but rather a circle whose sectors and segments together made up a social order. It was precisely her variety which gave Europe her sense of unity. The Greek geographer Strabo praised Europe for her variety, and it was to the contest between her various dynasties, States and peoples that Europe owed her finest achievements. Moreover, she knew how to absorb the contributions of alien cultures and to assimilate them into her own civilization. All the conflicts, disputes and wars which occurred in Europe were regarded as the affairs of members of one and the same family. Events outside this circle only concerned the members of the family if they were called upon to give judgement as referees. When this happened, they mostly acted independently of one another and only rarely did they co-operate. However, they were able at all times, thanks to their superior power, to maintain their position – at times at one another's expense and frequently in a mutual struggle for the division of the world.

All important ideas destined to grow into movements are either of European origin or they received their decisive initial impulse from Europe. This applies to democracy, Christianity, nationalism, Marxism, socialism and communism. Europe – geographically merely an appendix of Asia and ethnologically a highly imprecise concept – was to make its impact thanks to its virtually unlimited power for both good and evil. And since too much of a good thing tends to be bad, the 'isms' which Europe developed in vast numbers became the root cause of her own divisions. It is impossible to discuss this evolution without giving at least a rough outline of European history, if only because the problems which are of fundamental importance to the Europe of today cannot be viewed in isolation but must be considered in their historical context and as part of the processes of history, for if these problems are to be solved at all they must be solved by men who understand and are aware of these contexts and processes.

Europe, to put it simply, remained for nearly a thousand years a loose association of, above all, the Western nations settled in the region stretching from Scandinavia to Sicily and from Ireland to Russia. Even Russia was regarded as a part of Europe for many centuries although, owing to the vastness of her territory, the peculiar link between her form of government and her religion and the life of her people (moulded as it was by their Orthodox faith and their Euro-Asiatic background), she occupied a special position. The fact remains that until the Bolshevik revolution Russia was part of the Occident by virtue of her dynastic and cultural links. As for the West itself, it remained essentially Christian despite its political rifts and religious schisms and its ensuing secularization.

The geographical limits of Europe, bounded as she was by Ireland in the west and the Urals in the east, did not always coincide throughout the course of history with our concept of Europe as a cultural entity. For a time, the Mongols, the Magyars and the Turks pushed the European cultural sphere back from the east and the Saracens from the south-west, but finally these invaders were driven back, though some of them became absorbed into the European sphere. The Magyars, in fact, eventually became the protectors of Europe.

At no time, however, was Europe a political unit in the modern sense of the word. The mediaeval emperors, who considered themselves to be heirs to the Roman Empire, did not aim at extending their power over the whole of Europe; their principal goal was the politico-religious consolidation of the Italian-German area with the maintenance of their hegemony over the adjoining territories.

From the outset, Europe's history was marked by tensions.

3

The great conflict between the Emperors and the Popes was later replaced by disputes between the princes and their coalitions within the Holy Roman Empire as well as by the struggle between the imperial power on the one hand and the emerging territorial and dynastic States – only some of which were later to become the nation States of the future – on the other.

At first the Catholic, and later also the Protestant, Church provided spiritual leadership, with the Catholic Church emphasizing universalism and the Protestant particularism. The perpetuation of the Greco-Roman cultural heritage played just as important a part in this connection as the provision of spiritual and religious guidance. The wars of religion and the collapse of church unity marked the end of theology as the decisive force in Western civilization. Its place was taken by philosophy and science. A reaction to the earlier predominance of the Church set in, almost inevitably: an increasingly marked turning away from the doctrine which maintained that life is but a preparation, and must be guided by concern, for the hereafter. The age of enlightenment placed its faith in human reason, and the French Revolution translated this philosophy into a programme of political action.

How did the European States originate? In seeking to answer this question we must be clear from the outset that ethnical considerations, common origin or even linguistic kinship hardly played any part in the beginning. Dynastic aspirations and alliances exercised a much greater influence.

It is clear from the documents of the Congress of Vienna, for instance, how much haggling took place there – of a kind we may think rather repulsive nowadays – over the division of Poland as well as over such deals as the cession of Saxon territory to Prussia, the exchange of territories between Austria and Bavaria and the Netherlands-Prussian Treaty. I need hardly add that in all these arrangements economic assets, communications and, last but not least, strategic considerations played an important part. For instance, in return for Thorn (Torun) Prussia renounced Leipzig. She also accepted a British offer, put forward by Lord Castlereagh, that she should give up certain of her demands regarding the Prussian-Saxon frontier in return for two areas, with a population of fifty thousand each, which had originally been earmarked for the Netherlands and Hanover. To begin with, there was no such thing as nationalism: In many States, the most disparate populations, with some groups even differing as to language, lived side by side.

To take some German examples. In the South, the Hapsburg monarchy, comprising many nations, gradually began to take shape; in the North, in Prussia, groups of settlers from all the German regions amalgamated with populations already living there as well as with later arrivals, some of whom did not even originally speak German. Even during the period in which the first nation States of today began to take shape and when States with absolute forms of government were struggling for power, there was an awareness, especially among the nobility and the educated classes, of a common heritage – an awareness which at times took the form of cosmopolitanism.

In the first volume of his European history of the nineteenth century, Franz Schnabel quotes Dante's words – which show that there is a link between Dante himself and the stoics – about the wise man *cui mundus est patria ut piscibus aequor*. Schnabel goes on to say:

Throughout all the struggles for power which took place between its States, Europe remained in being as a spiritual and cultural unit. In fact, this awareness of a common destiny was to become even more marked with the advance of rationalist thinking, which came to discount more and more all differences of national characteristics, customs and taste until, finally, Rousseau was able to say of his own time: *Il n'y a plus que des Européens*. The natural law promoted the unity of the West, and once the wars of religion were over Christianity and humanism sought to create a human civilization embracing all the nations.

At the same time, however, an internal break-up of the European world occurred because, despite the fact that the nobility and the educated sections of the community were inspired by a feeling of kinship, there were then no political concepts in existence on which to base a spiritual or political order with a definite scale of values that could have acted as a motive force for European unity. This process of dissolution reached its climax in the French Revolution. Though the latter resulted in the virtual collapse of the old States, new forces emerged, some of which made their peace with the existing political structures while the others vanquished

5

them completely and struck out for new shores. The period 1914–45 marked the end of this process and brought with it a disaster which all but became mankind's final apocalypse.

The nineteenth century was the century of the bourgeois, of industrial technology, of liberal, constitutional parliamentary democracy and of European imperialism. It was the century, too, of the right of self-determination and of the centrifugal tendencies which found their expression in the three concepts of 'nation, State, power'. Here, too, we have the beginning of the chain which stretches from the nation State, via the Great Power and World Power to the power bloc, with one World Power predominating and providing strategic backing for the entire system.

Up to the Napoleonic era the European balance of power owed its existence to British efforts. It was a balance that was chiefly based on five capitals: London, Paris, Vienna, Berlin and St Petersburg – the pentarchy of European States. The Congress of Vienna was to restore this balance, within which only 'local disturbances' occurred up to the outbreak of the first world war, as we now realize when we measure these conflicts against the cataclysms which we have experienced in our generation. True, a whole series of crises and wars, revolutions and other disorders did occur during that century, but there were no catastrophes of historic dimensions. The Congress of Vienna did not create any international or supranational institutions. What it did do – if I may use an expression which has become fashionable – was to create a 'Europe of States', designed to be self-sufficient because it was internally balanced. Even defeated France was allotted a secure and acknowledged position within the European balance of power. The sovereignty of the States remained untouched. Europe relied on the solidarity of her monarchs and on their common desire to prevent any one of them from achieving a position of supremacy or hegemony. The victors of 1814–15 succeeded, in their wisdom, in creating a peace which, though not total or everlasting, was nevertheless better than the settlements of 1918 and 1945. They were able to do this because they did not rely solely on their military successes, because they did not think in terms of onesided moral categories and judgements and because they were careful not to attempt to establish a Thomas Moretype utopia in Europe.

6

A break in this era occurred during the period 1848–9, when there was a clash between the prevailing order and the new ideas which had become popular. But this clash did not result in the collapse of the existing order. The liberal bourgeois movement which emerged around the middle of the nineteenth century affected all the five Powers, including Russia. However, it did not destroy the community of the European dynasties because, in view of their common interests, they strove, and strove successfully, to hold down the new nationalist movements of the modern type.

Bismarck considered the continued existence of the European balance of power both natural and necessary. Thus he did everything he could after his victory over Austria to maintain that State as a great European Power and to preserve it from the indignity of an entry of Prussian troops into Vienna and from territorial losses. He adopted the same approach towards France, although, hard pressed by the military during the peace negotiations with France – which had not been the case during the negotiations with Austria – he reacted more sharply. This he was later to regret. In this connection it should be recalled that, in response to insistent demands by the General Staff, the fortress of Metz, the eastern part of Lorraine as well as the whole of Alsace, were ceded to the German Reich in 1871 by the Peace of Frankfurt because it was thought that Germany must secure these concessions both for a possible offensive deployment of her troops and in order to be able to set up a defensive screen.

During the course of the nineteenth century, four forces exerted an ever-increasing influence on political life: technology, nationalism, capitalism and socialism. According to Ortega y Gasset, three stages are to be distinguished in mankind's technological development:

1. The technology of chance. Primitive man determines his technological conduct by accident and through experience.

2. The technology of handicraft, which spread from Greece to pre-imperial Rome and hence into mediaeval Europe. Throughout its existence, there was an interplay of technology and politics – and this state of affairs continued right into the period of the corporate states of the peoples.

3. The technology of the technician. The invention of the

7

machine results in the replacement of manual labour by manufacture; craftsmen and technicians become one and the same and large-scale technology is born. Man becomes aware that his powers of invention are seemingly unlimited. The influence of technology on society, politics and warfare grows.

We are now in the stage of the technology of the technician; to mention but one example: the applications and possibilities of the computer. The vast populations of Europe now depend entirely on technical innovation and development, which are the conditions of rapid progress. It took Europe from the fifth century to the year 1800 – i.e. a period of thirteen centuries – to reach a population total of 180 million. This figure rose to 600 million from 1800 to 1900, and the process is continuing in arithmetical progression despite the heavy losses Europe sustained in the first and second world wars. If technology were to experience a setback – e.g. as a result of a nuclear war or some other disaster of cosmic proportions – hundreds of millions of people would lose their livelihood. During the last third of the nineteenth century technology grew into a sort of super-nature. The growth of Europe's population gave rise to numerous points of friction. Capitalism was in control; it consolidated the existing States and imparted imperialist impulses to them. In the meantime, Bismarck's Reich had come into being. At the time, within the frontiers it then had, it represented the utmost that Europe could be expected to tolerate, and Bismarck was well aware of this. Hence it was his aim, once the Reich had been founded, merely to consolidate it and to protect it from external danger. He had no intention of expanding the Reich or extending the area subject to its influence. This became clear when Britain began to support France immediately after Sedan, having previously pursued a policy favourable to Prussia in regard to the latter's power and influence within Germany. It was only thanks to the cautious policy of the Reich Chancellor that the *cauchemar des coalitions* did not there and then become a reality in response to the Reich's growing strength.

Once Bismarck was overthrown, the fatal policy was adopted which eventually led the neighbours of the Central Powers to draw together. Wilhelm II believed himself strong enough to be able to indulge in a 'policy of the free hand'. He did not renew the reinsurance treaty with Russia; he irritated Britain by his excessive naval construction programme and his schemes for economic expansion such as the Baghdad Railway, while he annoyed France with the Agadir 'Panther leap' incident. As a result, armies were created of a size never seen before. The militarization of Europe can be said to have begun at the turn of the century. At the same time, nationalism was making an even more marked impact than during the preceding period. The magnitude of the armaments programmes in hand profoundly influenced diplomatic relations. Nevertheless, Europe still held together, e.g. in the Boxer Rebellion in China. It was still possible to cross frontiers without passports and visas, and currencies remained freely convertible. Only to cross the Russian frontier was it necessary to have a passport. However, even this was largely due to Russian domestic considerations: the aim was to protect the tsarist throne. While Europeans were active throughout the world, the military and political situation in Europe itself, on the other hand was, in strange contrast, confined by tensions which had by now become very marked. The Reich had grown so powerful that, once the fatal shots had rung out in Sarajevo, Europe literally slithered into the first world war.

In that war, Europe showed no scruples in using her ample resources to destroy herself. Any one of the European Powers would, during the period from 28 June to 1 August 1914, either by acts of commission or omission, have been able to break the vicious circle before the explosion actually occurred. The conflict that began in 1914 was not a planned war; on the contrary, as George Ball says in his recently published book *The Discipline of Power*: 'It was the classically unique case of a tragic conflict caused by muddle and miscalculation.' Finally, the Americans came to the aid of the Allies when Russia's collapse appeared imminent and the Central Powers seemed to be on the verge of victory.

The outcome of the first world war was a complete shift in the balance of power. As a result of the collapse of the Hapsburg monarchy and the Ottoman Empire, as well as of the virtual demilitarization of Germany, a vacuum came into being in Central and Eastern Europe which was only tolerable because the Soviet Union was unable to become an effective power as a result of the

9

revolutionary turmoil in Russia. The communist advance failed at the gates of Warsaw; the communist rebellion in Germany was defeated. France established her European system at Versailles and St Germain, based on co-operation with the Little Entente and, in particular, with Poland. America, on the other hand, having only recently decisively intervened in European affairs and decided the outcome of the first world war, was soon to withdraw from Europe. The influence the USA exercised during the peace negotiations fell short of the hopes which had been raised by Wilson's Fourteen Points.

Efforts were made to find a 'modern solution' for the pacification and consolidation of Europe. The answer was to be the League of Nations – a supranational organization and a community over and above the States. The concept was not new; it can be traced back down the centuries to the ideas which gained currency here and there after the collapse of the mediaeval ideal of the Holy Roman Empire. (P. Dubois, Campanella, Sully, Kant, Görres, Novalis and Leibniz.) These ideas were concerned, above all, with the problem of whether there can be such a thing as 'eternal peace'. The impulse came from President Woodrow Wilson. The idea owes much to the Anglo-Saxon concept of peace and has strong puritanical undertones. The League of Nations was to exercise a centripetal counter-influence to the centrifugal tendencies which were inevitably triggered off by the application of the right of self-determination, especially in Eastern and South-Eastern Europe.

The Anglo-Saxon sponsors of the right of self-determination were, of course, influenced, above all, by the ideal expressed in the American Constitution which says that every government must have the consent of those governed and that territorial boundaries must not be changed without the agreement of those affected. The authors of this policy had little idea of the forces which were bound to be unleashed, first in the territories of the former Austro-Hungarian, and subsequently the Ottoman, Empires. Further complications arose as a result of the promise that had been given that these principles would be applied vis-à-vis the vanquished in a most 'generous' manner.

Thus we find the following elements side by side when the League of Nations came to be created: the ideal of a lasting peace; an almost blind faith in the viability of the right of self-determination in each and every case (with, underlying this faith, the optimistic idea that this was the lost key to the *harmonia praestabilita*); the idea that, on the one hand, collective security and, on the other, bilateral and multilateral alliances are easily compatible; finally, the dream that individuals and peoples would, in making political decisions, conduct themselves in accordance with Western ethical imperatives and in a rational manner, i.e. that they would prove themselves both good and pure.

In this connection, it is noteworthy that it was not a European but an African statesman who at that time, just as later in the second world war, had a better grasp of the problems, ideas and requirements of his time than any of his contemporaries in Europe and America. In his essay 'The Ideal and Concept of the Supranational State', Theodor Schieder notes that Smuts was probably the only allied statesman who had clearly proclaimed that the League of Nations must take the place of the former great empires, Russia, Austria-Hungary and Turkey. Smuts had stressed that the overthrow of the old empires must not be allowed to leave a vacuum in which national egotism and anarchy could assert themselves. Room must be made for a comprehensive and better 'League of Nations'. Smuts had also pointed to the great dangers which would ensue if Europe were to be split up again into its 'original atoms'.

From all this it is obvious which problems the League of Nations was unable to solve. The League could provide an answer to many minor questions; it could also discuss major problems, bridge differences and resolve crises, but it was bound to fail when asked to tackle the problems of major import. The League of Nations was beset by this weakness from its very inception, since its aims and possibilities could not be reduced to a common denominator in view of the conflicting objectives of its members and the resources at the League's disposal.

Europe witnessed the establishment of dictatorships pursuing imperialist aims. The first world war, which had been fought to 'make the world safe for democracy' (H. G. Wells, 1914), resulted in the monster of dictatorship raising its ugly head: first dictatorship of the proletariat in Russia, then – leaving aside the semi-dictatorships in such East European countries as Poland and Lithuania – the fascist dictatorship in Italy and, finally, Hitler's dictatorship in Germany. The rise of these dictatorships marked the zenith and subsequent demise of the European nation States. Again and again attempts were made during major crises to save the situation by carrying outmoded principles to new extremes. In actual fact, all the nationalisms found themselves in a blind alley at such moments of crisis. The League of Nations finally foundered due to the following causes: its possibly Utopian aims; the contradiction between its theory and practice; the failure of the USA to join it; the European victors' lack of vision and skill in fashioning a viable peace settlement, and the nationalistic imperialism of the dictatorships.

As for the Soviet Union, it counted on wars breaking out among the capitalist Powers and relied on this to help it along the way to world revolution and world domination. It had originally placed great hopes in the revolutionary zeal of the German workers. Britain believed that Europe could tackle its problems unaided; however, the forces which had assumed power in Russia and Germany no longer regarded Europe as an aim in itself but merely as a means to an end.

The situation in Europe and the world at that time has been strikingly and aptly described by George Ball:

The harsh truth is that, because Europeans had ceased to believe in themselves, Europe was morally sick. The prevailing mood of Britain and France was a compound of cynicism and fatalism and fatigue. In Paris, the watchword of the day was '*il faut en finir*' – reflecting the sinking sense of a world poised before chaos. In Britain, in that tense August of 1939, a harassed Prime Minister Neville Chamberlain remarked wearily to a friend, 'Every time Hitler occupies a country, he sends me another message.' . . .
. . . Nor did we Americans show any more sense. The mood on our side of the Atlantic was one of sheer escapism. Pretending to be asleep under the bedclothes, we turned our faces to the wall. We rejected the obligations of great power until the Japanese military made up our minds for us by attacking Pearl Harbor. Yet even that classic imbecility might not have saved us from a destructive period of division and debate, if Hitler had not resolved our doubts by declaring war.

The misconception of British pacifism, based on the noble but mistaken belief that disarmament – and if need be unilateral disarmament – is in itself a means to greater security continued to be publicized and practised years after Hitler's assumption of power. Hitler's breaches of the peace, his unilateral measures, as well as Italy's war of aggression against Ethiopia, met with nothing worse than moral indignation. The sanctions against Italy can be disregarded in this context because of their almost deliberate inefficacity. Hitler had a wonderfully acute political instinct for the weaknesses of the European edifice and made use of them without scruple. He demolished that edifice, which it had taken centuries to create, once and for all. Dean Acheson said in a speech in 1963 that these conflicts had resulted in changes such as had not been seen since the collapse of the Roman Empire: 'This civil war destroyed the six great empires – the British, French, German, Austro-Hungarian, Ottoman and Russian – which had, thanks to their co-operation and equilibrium, supplied balance and order to the lives of the peoples. It was this collapse which opened up the way for the Russian and Chinese revolutions.'

The result of the second world war was the destruction of Europe. After the first world war – despite the fact that its outcome was decided during its final phase by the Americans – it was the statesmen or, to be more exact, the national politicians of Europe who made the decisions about the armistice and the peace. But at the end of the second world war it was non-European statesmen who made the decisions. Europe had become a chess-board for the non-European Powers. A distinct line led from Versailles via Hitler to Yalta and Potsdam. Symbolically, the line ended at the point where the American and Russian troops met on the banks of the Elbe at Torgau in April 1945. *Finis Germaniae* and *finis Europae?*

Not a single European continental Power took part in the main conferences which determined the postwar fate of Europe – Tehran, Yalta and Potsdam. Sir Winston Churchill, Britain's leading statesman, more than once felt that Europe was threatened but his government was relegated to the position of a junior partner beside the two Super-Powers. Though the members of the unnatural alliance which had been brought into being by Hitler had common war aims, they had anything but common peace aims.

The Soviet Union was not prepared, throughout the duration of the war, to make the slightest concession regarding its own aims and objectives. Its inflexible intention was, once it had become clear after the great German defeat at Stalingrad that it would eventually emerge victorious, to prevent the rise of a counter-vailing force in Central Europe and to apply all available political and military means to this end. It was the aim of the USSR to push Western influence as far back to the periphery of the European land mass as possible.

The Western allied leaders had no clear idea of the sort of Europe they wished to see come into being after the war. The political and military elimination of Germany, if not for always then for a long time to come, was to serve two objectives:

1. The Soviet Russian ally was to be eased into a peaceful and friendly mood through the implementation of most of its wishes.

2. Lasting peace was to be safeguarded with virtually math-ematical certainty through the elimination of Germany, supposedly the only instigator of war in the world.

In this way, through a radical abandonment of the traditional forms of diplomacy in European political life, the very concept of self-determination for the peoples of Eastern and South-Eastern Europe was sacrificed, if not formally then in actual fact, and was henceforth made the object of lip service only. All this was done in the hope of ensuring the smooth functioning of military co-operation with the Soviet Union. The invasion of Central Europe by the Soviet Russians is the historic catastrophe of our century. It was Hitler's criminal, megalomaniac policy which opened the door to them, and the allies were not strong enough to close that door in time.

As after the first world war, clearly defined peace aims and a firm resolve to ensure their implementation were replaced by the notion that all the ideals which had, in their time, been conceived by the initiators of the League of Nations, could be attained through the foundation of a new supranational organization and community of States. This belief was thought to be the more justified as not only nearly all the medium and small Powers from the outset belonged to that organization – the United Nations – but, above all the only two remaining World Powers, the United States and the Soviet Union. At that point in time there were only two genuine Great Powers left in the world – the USA and the USSR – and this situation persists in essence to this day.

# 2  *Fresh Start and 'Containment'*

The error underlying the notion that the United Nations could be made into a genuine precursor of a world State was based in good part on a wrong assessment of Soviet strategic aims. And yet, the West, and especially Washington, should have known that the 'one world' ideal, the concept of a global democracy based on free and peaceful co-operation, had no place in the Soviet philosophy of history. According to the latter, mankind must inevitably pass through several stages, predetermined by a law of history. They are: the primitive-nomadic stage; the feudal-dynastic stage; and the capitalist-imperialist-colonialist stage; finally, with the inexorable force of destiny, comes the stage of socialism, culminating in the classless and stateless communist order of society.

According to the Soviet view, the course of history is predetermined, i.e. history is merely a sequence of events which follow one another in a preordained manner, although, of course, these events must be assisted with countless measures taken at one's own initiative. As for the historians, their task is merely to draw up a record of the unfolding of this law of development. This thought was expressed by a contemporary Russian author, Alexey Tolstoy, in his novel *The Road to Calvary* in these words, which occur in a dialogue:

Do you remember, comrade, we have discussed this quite a bit – this tiresome fact that history goes round and round, that great civilizations have to go under and great ideas turn into miserable parodies of themselves.... But it's all lies! I can now see it all clearly ... a brilliant light has been shed on the half-destroyed arches of past centuries. There is harmony and order in everything; all events are governed by a law.... Our goal is clear ... every Red Army man is aware of it ...

15

This is why the prophets and apostles of communism are quite familiar with the idea of a 'world State'. According to them, that State is being created through the process of permanent and expanding world revolution, and the final victory of communism throughout the world over its external and internal enemies will mark the completion of the new 'State' – which will in fact no longer be a State as we understand it.

It is entirely in keeping with this line of thought that the Soviets, after the first world war, at first refused to join the League of Nations. Unlike the United States, it was not isolationist tendencies which prevented the Soviets from joining the League but disagreements about what the latter's aims and functions should be. People's Commissar Chicherin declared in a Note to President Wilson on 24 October 1918 in which he discussed ways to improve the League: 'The League of Nations should not only put an end to the present war, it should make all wars impossible in the future. . . . We therefore propose, Mr President, that the League of Nations be founded on the principle of the expropriation of the capitalists of all countries.' As a counter-move to the establishment of the League of Nations, Lenin set up the 'Comintern', which was later to be disbanded, during the second world war, to deceive the Western allies. The task of that organization was to work for the establishment of a communist 'world State'. It is worth noting that Moscow was made the headquarters of the Comintern on a temporary basis only since it was thought that its permanent seat would eventually be in Berlin once conditions had become right for such a move. Two leading communists, Bukharin and Preobrazhensky, described the League of Nations in their *ABC of Communism* as a 'league of bandits' whose aim it was to set up a 'capitalist world State corporation'. They went on to say that

the League of Nations can be seen as an attempt to establish an immense worldwide trust embracing the entire earth. It is to exploit the whole world while, at the same time, suppressing the working class and its revolution with the utmost brutality. All talk about the League of Nations guaranteeing peace is so much nonsense. . . . But the League of Nations will not attain its twin objectives – to organize the world economy as a single trust and completely to suppress the revolution. The Great Powers are not sufficiently united to achieve these aims.

In the years that followed, the Soviets vigorously attacked all plans for a supranational association of States. Thus, they assailed the scheme for a Pan-Europe devised by Count Coudenhove-Kalergi, which later re-emerged, during the course of League of Nations debates, in Briand's proposal for a loose working community of sovereign European States. Eventually, the scheme fell victim to the tough realities of the early thirties. Europe had missed her finest chance. The fact that this opportunity was allowed to go by default was due not so much to the objective conditions in Europe as to a lack of subjective spiritual and moral fibre and intellectual vision on the part of the leaders responsible for the future of Europe, who were beset by worries about the economic situation and the political vagaries of the day – dependent as they were on coalitions and the state of domestic politics.

The Soviet reaction to another proposal – this time by a private individual – for the establishment of a federation of the Western democracies is particularly interesting. The total failure of the League of Nations vis-à-vis the Great Powers and the serious political problems and crises of the time induced Clarence Streit, in March 1939, to publish his appeal *Union Now*. He said that war was imminent because the Western democracies were weak and disunited in facing up to the powers of aggression. Goodman noted in the spring of 1939 that this weakness marred every League of Nations system from the outset since these systems depended on a continuous and unanimous agreement of all member States if they were to unite in common action; however, these member States insisted on their sovereign rights as members of a splintered community. Only through the establishment of a common government which would be in a position to take positive and united action could the Western democracies be adequately defended. Moreover, a federation of the Western democracies around the shores of the North Atlantic (the United States, the members of the British Commonwealth, the democracies of continental Europe and Scandinavia) would immensely strengthen the democratic institutions of the world, give rise to new productive forces within a huge common market and provide a soil in which personal liberty could thrive. This union of free nations could at the same time serve as the nucleus for an eventual world union of democratic States. When one considers the efforts that are being made at the present time, one can but ask oneself what would have happened if. ... But there is little point in such unrealistic speculation.

In September 1939, the Soviet Union had no intention of preventing a war between Germany and the Western democracies, and it was therefore deaf and dumb to all plans aimed at averting such a war. This is clear from an official commentary which appeared in the publication *Comintern*.* This said:

> The ideologists of big business are now trying to persuade the peoples that war must be waged in order to promote the creation of a super-empire of all the democratic 'States' and thus to establish the basis of a lasting peace. This idea is being hawked around as an entirely new product, but in reality it has been lying about on the shelves of imperialism for a long time. ... Any such super-empire, far from guaranteeing peace, would merely create a machine which would give rise to a new war.

However, after the second world war, Stalin took up Roosevelt's favourite idea and declared himself ready to join a United Nations Organization from the outset. In return, Stalin obtained important concessions from Roosevelt, who attached great value to Soviet Russia's agreement, concessions which were not confined to the granting of three votes to the Soviet Union in the United Nations Assembly. What happened in practice was that one of the war aims which had played a decisive part both in the first and second world wars – the East and South-East European peoples' right to self-determination – was sacrificed, perhaps not deliberately from the outset but in any case later under the impact of the harsh realities of the situation.

Apart from wishing to pocket this little 'dowry', what were the motives of the Soviet Union in consenting to join the United Nations ? Was the USSR genuinely prepared to give up its former aims regarding a communist 'world State' ? Was it genuinely prepared to come to an understanding with the non-communist world, an understanding involving a gradual transformation of the communist social and governmental institutions ? Or were there other motives ?

Three objectives can be discerned:

1. The principle of unanimity of the Great Powers in all matters

*Vol. 16, No. 11, November 1939

before the Security Council, in accordance with the UN Charter, meant that any outside intervention regarding conditions within the Soviet sphere of influence could be precluded in advance thanks to the Soviet Union's power of veto. In the Korean war, it was only due to the fact that the USSR had absented itself from the Security Council that the United States was able to intervene under the UN flag.

2. The UN offered the Soviets an excellent opportunity for gaining political influence in the non-communist world and enabled it to play a prominent part in UN measures to deal with crises outside the Soviet sphere of influence.

3. The UN has all along offered the USSR an excellent chance of exploiting the desire of the coloured peoples, especially the former colonial nations, for national freedom and of presenting itself as the main champion of the struggle against colonialism. The assumption that the balance of voting strength within the UN would gradually change in favour of the coloured world and that this would benefit the USSR is also bound to have played a part in its calculations.

At no time did the Soviet Union have any thought of genuinely according to the United Nations supranational powers, and it has always strenuously opposed all attempts aimed at depriving the Security Council – where all decisions must be taken unanimously by the Great Powers plus two co-opted members – of the right to deal with security matters and transferring that privilege to some other body, e.g. a restricted UN Assembly or the full Assembly, where a qualified majority would suffice to carry a motion. The Soviet Union simply has never had the slightest desire to see either such a restricted Assembly or a full UN Assembly empowered to take decisions affecting problems of security.

It was soon to become patently obvious – in view of the attitude of the USSR – that the UN was powerless to establish a peaceful order in the world. Moscow looked upon its military conquests as historic changes in the situation in accordance with the doctrine of historical materialism. What was considered by the West to be imperialist expansion was regarded by the Soviets as part of the 'forward march' of the world revolution, first in Europe and later also in Asia. The destroyed continent of Europe, where the devastation of war had left victors and vanquished almost equally destitute, was regarded by Moscow as the ideal field for a chain action and reaction which was to facilitate a communist seizure of power. If they could lay their hands on defeated Germany – so the Kremlin strategists thought, encouraged, no doubt, by Roosevelt's naivety vis-à-vis the Soviets and his ignorance of European history – the whole of Europe would in due course be theirs. Germany was divided into four occupation zones; her industries were largely ruined and their remnants dismantled. Ten million refugees from the East German regions had flooded into the area plus millions of others who had left the Soviet zone of occupation for the West. On the face of it, all this seemed to provide an ideal breeding ground for the conditions needed to facilitate a communist seizure of power from within. The strong Communist Parties of France and Italy were ready to support a communist advance to the Atlantic.

From the communist point of view, it was a matter of course that in virtually all the States and territories into which the Red Army had advanced communist societies would be established. As for the West, it ought not to have expected anything else, since this Soviet attitude was entirely in keeping with Soviet beliefs. The notion that Soviet troops would protect and guarantee the functioning of a democratic system of government was utterly fantastic. A Western-type society, existing and flourishing under Soviet control, would have been a monster and would have been considered politically and ideologically suicidal by the communists themselves. Stalin was quite consistent in extending his territorial system up to the limits which the West had set for the advance of the Red Army. Austria (and also Azerbaijan and parts of Finland) were merely exceptions to this rule – exceptions which the Russians accepted in accordance with the dictum 'one step backward, two steps forward'.

The European view of the situation as it then was cannot be described more aptly or succinctly than was done at the time by Paul-Henri Spaak: 'One hundred and sixty million Europeans are living on the charity of a hundred and sixty million Americans and in fear of two hundred million Russians.'

And yet, once again there seemed to be a fresh chance: In his great speech to the students of Zürich, Winston Churchill outlined a plan for a better future of our continent:

... There is a remedy which, if it were generally and spontaneously adopted, would as if by a miracle transform the whole scene, and would in a few years make all Europe, or the greater part of it, as free and as happy as Switzerland is today. What is this sovereign remedy? It is to re-create the European Family, or as much of it as we can, and provide it with a structure under which it can dwell in peace, in safety and in freedom. We must build a kind of United States of Europe. ...

... The first step in the re-creation of the European family must be a partnership between France and Germany. ... There can be no revival of Europe without a spiritually great France and a spiritually great Germany.

Churchill was voicing the thoughts of many Europeans. In all the countries of Europe, people from all walks of life had begun to join forces in order to take stock of the spiritual and political situation. They were looking for a way out of the chaos. Among the young people of all countries feeling was running high in favour of a united Europe. They held tumultuous demonstrations and removed frontier posts to express their desire for a common European fatherland. Fortunately, however, the lesson of past failures had been well learnt. It was realized that the pursuit of an ideal must not be allowed to obscure the facts, that progress must be sought patiently, step by step, if the distant goal were to be reached. For the unification of Europe was not a spiritual task – it was, in the first instance, a political undertaking which could not be accomplished by displays of temper or emotional scenes. The 'Europeans' in the various countries, who were more cautious than the young in appraising the situation and planning for the future, were agreed on the following points:

1. Europe can preserve her political independence between the great World Powers of America and Soviet Russia only if she closes her ranks politically, be it comparatively loosely as a federation of States, be it by means of the closer unity of a federal State. The likelihood was that this sequence would in fact be followed.

2. Europe can only maintain its cultural position in the world if her peoples come to realize anew that they have a common heritage, which they must be prepared to live up to, cultivate and develop together.

3. Europe can only defend herself against the threat of

21

aggressive communism if she unites and consolidates her political, economic and military resources.

4. Many of her tasks Europe can accomplish only if her peoples strive together to rebuild their ruined economic resources.

No one doubted that this last point was the most urgent to begin with. To keep Europe alive, the Americans, who were well aware of their European roots, provided, during the first three postwar years, fifteen thousand million dollars' worth of food, medical supplies, consumer goods and raw materials. This state of affairs, however, could not possibly be allowed to continue, for in each of her hundred and sixty million citizens, Europe possessed an invaluable reserve of knowledge, skill and energy. All she needed was a booster charge to get the European engine to fire.

George Marshall, US Secretary of State, declared in a speech to the students of Harvard in June 1947 that Europe should be given substantial additional aid or she would face an extremely grave economic, social and political crisis. He insisted that this vicious circle should be broken and the confidence of the peoples of Europe in the economy of the various countries – and in that of the whole of Europe – restored. Before the United States continued its efforts, and in order that it might be able to contribute to the process of Europe's rehabilitation, he advocated that the countries of Europe should decide among themselves what was most urgently required in the prevailing situation and what the countries of Europe could do for themselves so that maximum advantage might be taken of the United States Government's measures.

The fact that the three Western occupation zones were included in this aid programme provided a striking contrast to the Morgenthau Plan, inspired as the latter was by thirst for revenge. All this – now mostly forgotten – is, I think, worth recalling because it shows that Europe's fresh start received its initial impulse from America and that it was the latter which made possible the rebuilding of our continent. Through its aid, America gave us a chance to realize our hopes. The Marshall Plan was followed by the creation of the Council of Europe, the Organization for European Economic Co-operation (OEEC), the European Payments Union, the Steel and Coal Community, the European Economic Community (EEC) and Euratom – all ventures which, in their various ways and through their various members, seek to promote what we have come to call 'integration'. These are ventures which have spread economic prosperity, ventures which, even if it should prove impossible to expand them further, not one of the member countries would wish, or would be able to, liquidate.

Politically, however, Europe has not only made no real breakthrough but has achieved absolutely nothing. The treaty which was to have established the European Defence Community (EDC) and forged the unity of our part of the world in terms of security and defence policy, suffered shipwreck in 1954 in the French National Assembly. One of the main reasons was that Britain, her eyes fixed on her Commonwealth ties, did not wish the United Kingdom to merge with the continent. As a result, France – at grips, at that time, with wars in Indochina and Africa, anxious to assert herself after her defeat in 1940 and swayed hither and thither by memories of her former greatness and disappointments of her recent past – lacked the courage to enter into a direct military association with dynamic Germany. The West European Union was but an inadequate substitute for the EDC.

At that juncture, Europe threw away an historic opportunity. She failed to grasp her chance when it was beckoning, perhaps because she was still too weak at that time to do so. NATO, which was enlarged through the accession of the Federal Republic, helped to cover up the misfortune which had befallen Europe. Only a handful of people realized what had happened – Konrad Adenauer, for one, grasped the full extent of the disaster. Under the protective umbrella of the United States, Europe believed herself to be safe for all time. Though the ideal of political unity continued to be thought desirable, its realization was no longer regarded as a matter of urgency. Appearances certainly supported this view, for the political situation in Europe had become remarkably stable thanks to America's strategy of containment. It seemed that Soviet expansion had been halted for good. Let us cast our minds back to the course of events up to the end of the fifties.

In the first postwar phase, the Soviet Union sought to frustrate the establishment of the German Federal Republic. Subsequently, it tried to prevent the Federal Republic from concluding an alliance with the West, from becoming a military power in its own right, in fact a power factor of any kind within the Western camp.

23

The turning point in the relations between the four victorious Powers came at the Conference of Foreign Ministers in the autumn of 1946, when the Western attempt failed to achieve an understanding with the Soviet Union about the future of Germany on the basis of the Potsdam Agreement. The latter had laid it down that the four occupation zones were to be regarded as one administrative and economic unit. However, the Russians laid down three conditions for this: Firstly, they demanded reparations amounting to ten thousand million dollars out of current production – a wholly unrealistic sum. Secondly, they required that the Soviet Union be given the right to participate in the control of the Rhine-Ruhr area. Thirdly, they wished to see 'democratic, peaceful conditions' created in the Western occupation zones such as obtained in the communist-controlled zone. The West gave its reply in a speech by Burnes, US Secretary of State, in Stuttgart that same year – 1946. He announced a complete reorientation of American policy vis-à-vis Germany, Europe and the Soviet Union. This was followed by the policy of 'containment', pursued by Dean Acheson and John Foster Dulles through the expansion of NATO, itself established in 1949.

In the second phase of its postwar policy, the Soviet Union was forced to postpone its demands for influence and control over the whole of Germany. Since that time, it has suffered increasing setbacks and difficulties, especially since the emergence of Red China. In view of this, the USSR has thought it best to try to safeguard and obtain recognition for its sphere of influence. The Western Powers were to be persuaded formally to approve the status quo, to recognize the existence of 'two German States' and of a 'free city of West Berlin', as well as to guarantee the communist regimes in Poland, Czechoslovakia, Hungary and the other countries of Eastern Europe.

The goals set by communist ideology were thus not attained for the time being, and there was every indication that a war between the 'capitalist' countries had become unthinkable. Moscow's assumption had proved false that these countries would fall upon one another and thus lay themselves open to communist infiltration and invasion. Nor did the Afro-Asian world meet the expectations of Soviet strategy – at least not to the extent which the Soviet Union had hoped for. And yet a further setback was sustained by the Soviets. The 'masses' in the highly industrialized countries ceased to be a potential vehicle of world revolution, contrary to the predictions of Marx and Lenin. They no longer had to fight for a tolerable standard of living, for equal rights and privileges. In fact, they began to enjoy a standard of living which is certain to meet their rising demands as time goes on. There thus seemed to be no prospect of an expansion of communism westward by infiltration, military force or internal revolution. Such developments in Western Europe as outbreaks of violence with revolutionary undertones, staged by students – and disorders, of a very different type, by workers – all contain elements which, far from favouring the aims of the Soviets, fill the latter with misgivings, for these rebellions are either directed against all authority as such or they are aimed at winning social and political gains which, as events of the recent past have proved, the communist regimes are least able to provide.

# 3 From the Degeneration of War to the 'Pax Atomica'

The fact that our continent appears to be going through a period of tranquillity and the assumption that Europe is on the brink of a lasting peace, have given rise to the notion, occasionally expressed in so many words, that Britain and the countries of the Continent of Europe should take on the same role vis-à-vis the United States as was played by the Greeks in the Roman Empire during the first century BC. This parallel – however attractive it may seem on the face of it – is based on a number of false assumptions. Firstly, Washington is not a latter-day Rome and, secondly, the USA, which emerged from the second world war as a superpower, is not another Roman Empire. Thus, the Pax Romana of that time has no parallel in a twentieth century Pax Americana. In their day, the Romans held undivided sway over the whole of the civilized world, and their sole preoccupation was to keep the barbarians away from their frontiers. The last civil war between the nations of Europe was, however, won by two extra-European States, each the size of a continent. The postwar world was ruled, supervised and supported in a polarized system by the two superpowers. But these two Powers did not collectively exercise the function of ancient Rome. Instead, since the brief weeks of honeymoon which followed their victory, they have been facing each other in the sharpest possible disagreement, and this situation has remained unchanged to this day despite all the attempts that have been made by them to arrive at a settlement of their differences.

This division and polarization of the world was modified by the emancipation of the former colonial peoples, i.e. the emergence of the third world; the rise of Red China to the status of a future nuclear World Power and a rival to Moscow for leadership of the communist, as well as the coloured, world; de Gaulle's withdrawal from NATO, with which he was, in any case, never too closely associated; and the trend to independence within the Soviet sphere, for example in Rumania and Czechoslovakia. However, these polycentric tendencies do not mean that Europe is reverting to its former division into a multiplicity of States, for a new force has emerged which is changing the world. The second industrial revolution, brought about by the tremendous scientific-technical explosion that has taken place. The new industrial revolution has in every respect set new limits to the sovereignty of States. The extent to which a nation or State can approach these limits provides us with a yardstick with which to measure the extent of its independence and its freedom to manoeuvre in asserting its right to self-determination.

I now propose to diverge – though only seemingly – from our main theme and to give a brief outline of the changes which the phenomenon of 'war' has undergone, for only thus can Europe's situation and the possible developments and dangers which it may have to face in the future be explained. Armed conflict has always been considered an instrument of policy. It has helped the States to solve problems which could not be tackled in any other way. The Greeks, who coined the phrase 'war is the father of all things', invented the legend of the Gordian knot, which Alexander the Great is supposed to have cut in 333 BC in order to make himself the ruler over all Asia. The gun barrels of Louis XIV's armies were decorated with the inscription *Ultima Ratio Regum*. This was later altered by Frederick II of Prussia to *Ultima Ratio Regis* and displayed on his artillery colours and bronze guns. The inscription was taken from Calderon de la Barca, one of whose characters says in a play first shown in 1644 that powder and shot are the *ultima razon de reyes*.

It was left to the Prussian Karl von Clausewitz to define the political function of warfare with scientific precision. In his fragmentary work, which he completed during the years 1816–30, the general attempted to subject the struggle of the nations and States to a rational – one might almost say abstract – examination. Clausewitz drew his conclusions from his observations of the events of the eighteenth century. After the dreadful devastation of the preceding period, which included the Thirty Years War with its five million dead, these events had begun to conform to the *ultima ratio*. The strange notion that people can usually be made to listen to reason also dates back to this time and thus a development was set in motion which was eventually to have terrible consequences, with warfare inevitably degenerating into a 'senseless and useless thing'. Only a slight inkling of this danger entered the general's mind, though Goethe had realized even before Clausewitz that a new chapter had begun in the relations between nations. Describing the battle between the allied German troops and the French revolutionary army at Valmy in September 1792, he said: 'This day, a new era has begun in world history at this place, and you may claim to have been there. . . .'

The advance of the new epoch in world history mentioned by Goethe was, however, held up yet again for a time. Europe's armies underwent certain changes both during the Napoleonic Wars and in later years, thanks to a number of reforms, and the monarchies, which had been restored to power, had no scruples about adopting that 'true-born child of democracy', conscription. Nevertheless, the statesmen of the much-maligned nineteenth century succeeded in keeping warfare within bounds and under political control. They met Clausewitz's demand that even when exchanging the pen for the dagger they should make sure the military instrument was only used within the limits set by political considerations.

It may seem incredible to us in our day and age that in all the clashes of arms which occurred in the nineteenth century – an era which, when all is said and done, began with fifteen years of war, a mere four million people lost their lives. In the battles of the twentieth century – only two thirds of which have elapsed to date – the nations of the world have lost at least twenty-five times that number of lives. The German War of 1866 cost 30,000 lives, and the Franco-Prussian war of 1870–71 cost a total of 188,000 lives. By contrast, about 10 million people were killed in the 1914–18 war, and nearly 56 million in the second world war.

In the last century statesmen had not yet lost the art of treating peace as the ultimate aim of war, and victory was not imposed on the enemy the way one executes a criminal. Reason was allowed to remain in control of emotion. Certain quotations from Bismarck shed light, not only upon his own views but on those which were current in his time. He declared in 1866: 'If we do not go too far in our claims and do not delude ourselves into believing that we have conquered the world, we shall achieve a peace which will have been worth the effort. Unfortunately, we are just as apt to let ourselves be carried away as to be over-cautious, and it is my thankless task to pour water into the foaming wine and to make people realize that we are not alone in Europe but have three neighbours.' And he was to say later in the same year: 'We should never have achieved a peace settlement . . . if either of the two parties had been required to confess: "I realize now that I have acted wrongly." ' And Bismarck said in 1870: 'It can be no part of our business to punish a nation for a war waged by its government. It was not our task to impose just retribution; what we wanted to do was to act in a way that was right and useful to our nation.' In 1871 he declared: 'I do not consider it to be our task to inflict more damage upon our neighbour than is absolutely necessary to ensure implementation of the peace settlement. On the contrary, we should help him to recover from the disaster which has befallen his country, in so far as this can be done without prejudice to our interests.'

One of the reasons why the statesmen of Central Europe believed at that time that it was their duty to resist the advance of democracy was their fear of the emotions of the masses. They believed that once the masses had gained control over political events they might misuse that most dangerous of political instruments, war. These statesmen were very far from sharing the idealistic notion that wars of aggression and conquest are bound to become a thing of the past once the task of defence has been entrusted to the people. Present-day historians of Western Europe agree with this view of the risks inherent in popular government, though they do not necessarily approve the anti-democratic policies of the statesmen of those days. The British historian John Fuller noted in 1964: 'The motive power of democracy is not love of one's neighbour but hatred of all those who are outside one's own tribe, group, party or nation. Total war is based on the general will, and hate is its most powerful driving force.'

The fact is that the first total wars in the contemporary sense of that word were started 'by the will of the people'. At a time when Europe was still substantially managing to solve its problems by means of wisely and moderately conducted 'cabinet wars', popular passion was already raging in America. The 1861–65 Civil War in the United States, which resulted in the death of 620,000 people, was waged as a campaign of ruthless retribution by the North against the South. For the first time, the victor called for the 'unconditional surrender' of the vanquished – a modern version of the classical *vae victis* and a baneful omen for the future. During the years 1864–70, the Argentine, Brazil and Uruguay waged a ghastly war of extermination against Paraguay, which cost the lives of 1,300,000 people.

Though it would, of course, be wrong to believe that its 'democratization' was alone responsible for the degeneration of war, we should nevertheless do well to bear in mind that the rule of the people – particularly the Jacobin, totalitarian variants of it – does not in itself guarantee that military power will be used rationally. An example of this was provided by the Athenians in the Peloponnesian War. Democracy, besides its decisive advantages, on which we base our stand, has a disadvantage. It is that in a democracy irrational motives are apt to be given undue weight, especially in extreme situations. There is no doubt that man loves peace and therefore always considers that war has been forced upon him. Yet this is the very reason why he wishes to destroy his enemy – who is naturally always held responsible for the outbreak of war – and by destroying the enemy he wants to destroy all that is evil in order that good might at long last be allowed to prevail. Within the nations a kind of blind inebriation thus gains hold – the sum total of the fury of the individual members of the population – who then call upon the government to impose upon the enemy, if need be by the most brutal means conceivable, respect for the moral law. Any statesman bent on resisting this type of pressure should from the outset realize these risks in determining his policies.

However, the clock cannot be turned back by a hundred, let alone two hundred years. As Clausewitz predicted a hundred and forty years ago, war has always inevitably 'led to extremes' as a result of the mutual escalation of hostilities. The fact is that as long ago as the beginning of the twentieth century there were no longer any restrictions observed on the use of force. This was due to a number of facts and circumstances which had by then become too strong to be ignored. The development of modern industrial society, which according to Ernst Jünger allows the people 'to gain control of the potential energies of the nations', resulted in warfare becoming a law unto itself. It was no longer a case of armies going into battle at the behest of their governments, so that the conduct of war was a matter exclusively for the 'combatants', but whole nations were mobilized and the national economies became war economies – huge arsenals, in fact. The front line and the rear became one.

The 'population explosion' made available human material for war in quantities never before seen. Rome's standing army totalled 750,000 men in the fourth century AD; Wallenstein's forces had a mere 40,000 men in the year 1662; Prussia had 156,000 mercenaries in 1745, and Napoleon's Grande Armée totalled 450,000 infantry, cavalry, artillery and sappers in 1812. In mid-November 1870 – prior to the great battles on the Loire – some 425,000 Germans were facing 600,000 Frenchmen. In the first world war, the Central Powers mobilized in all 21,200,000 men, and the Allies some 39 million. In the second world war, Britain had 5,100,000 men under arms in 1945; the United States 8,300,000 and the German Reich 7,600,000, while the Soviet Union had 27 million troops at its disposal.

The revolution in conventional armaments created the machine gun, improved the fire power and range of the artillery, created the submarine and equipped the armed forces with aircraft. The range of conventional weapons was completed and perfected by means of tanks and rockets. The forces let loose on mankind even during the pre-nuclear era should have made the politicians and generals realize that there were no longer any war aims left worth pursuing, having regard to the inevitable cost.

Thus, in the first world war, what was to have been a rational application of the instrument of war turned into a frenzied carnage. And although the generals succeeded during the second world war in overcoming the rigidity of positional warfare and in restoring movement, the war as a whole offered a spectacle of devastation and massacre. It was a series of crusades: seen through German eyes, it was a campaign against 'plutocratic world Jewry' and 'Jewish bolshevism'; to the Russians it was a war against fascism and capitalism; and to the Western Powers a crusade against militarism and nazism. This view in no way detracts from the author's opinion that it is Hitler who must be held responsible, politically and morally, for the second world war, notwithstanding the fact that many others contributed to its outbreak by their sins both of commission and omission.

Warfare seemed to have reached the nadir of degeneration and to have become an 'act of blind passion' without any redeeming feature. It was two new factors, both of a scientific-technological nature, which towards the end of the second world war finally opened our eyes to the senselessness of war as such. I am referring to man's success in penetrating matter by splitting the atom (and also by fusing atomic nuclei into new elements), as well as to the first beginnings of man's penetration of space. It may well have been no coincidence that, after decades of effort, man's penetration of the microcosm and macrocosm occurred simultaneously. Forces and capabilities are being placed in man's hands which have hitherto been thought to belong to the Creator alone. Perhaps I might here recall the ancient legend of Prometheus, who was punished for stealing fire and giving it to man by being for ever shackled to the Caucasus, for fire was held to be a dangerous possession in the hands of man regardless of the great benefits it bestowed on him. What would a modern legend say, and how would he have to be punished who has placed the cosmic fire in the hands of man? The problem can no longer be solved by technical means, though it may still be brought under control by political methods, provided both sides are willing to submit their policies to a moral law whereby the forces of technology that have been unleashed would not merely serve their lust for power but would be subject to ethical considerations based on man's duty to God and himself. The same result can also be achieved, pending the attainment of the blissful state described above, so long as at least one side embraces this outlook and, moreover, shows sufficient will-power and moral determination to prevent the other from using this new capability for forbidden ends, including political blackmail.

As for time and distance, they no longer play any role in the world of today. The efficacy of the forces that have been unleashed, the possibility of bringing modern rocket technology to bear at any point of the globe at any time and, moreover, the possibility of leaving such devices circling in space, ready for use at any moment – all this should convince us that one phase in mankind's history is coming to an end and a new one is beginning, without anyone being able to predict what the end of it all will be.

The Portuguese discoverer Magellan took three years to sail round the world. In my father's and grandfather's time, Jules Verne's idea of a man going 'Round the World in Eighty Days' was considered sensational. Nowadays, it is technically feasible to fly round the world in twenty-four hours, and the time required for an intercontinental missile to reach the east coast of America from Central Russia at a speed of over 17,000 m.p.h. is thirty minutes. A satellite circles the earth in eighty to ninety minutes. The question we must ask ourselves is: Having regard to these changes, are our institutions still adequate?

If man, if *homo sapiens* were really an *animal rationale*, he would be bound to conclude that modern scientific research and the technological application of its results call for the formation of a world government now. It goes without saying that such a world organization would only be empowered to play a subsidiary role, i.e. it would have to confine itself to tackling problems which, in view of their complexity and the scope of the matters involved, could not be dealt with at a lower political level, the more so as the speed, range and fire power of modern weapons have made the world of today even smaller than Attica was 2,400 years ago. The world organization, of course, would not be permitted to intervene in the internal affairs of its various member States unless developments in a given State presented a danger to the rest or unless basic human rights were being violated in the State concerned. Unfortunately, however, the notion of a world government or world organization being created to solve supranational problems is bound to remain utterly Utopian so long as one side remains unalterably attached – even though we should dearly like to believe otherwise – to the communist view of history and of the world. However, our aim must be to create such an organization, not for its own sake but to establish the minimum of co-operation in order to secure respect for that most fundamental and essential of all principles, i.e. for a common, and universally respected, international law, observance or otherwise of which would then no longer be left to the whim of individual member States.

But the harsh facts of the situation carry more weight than any theories of moral philosophy, for any international law must remain a mere figment of the imagination, a mere hypothesis, in the absence of an executive power able to enforce it in the event of an attempted violation. Ernst Jünger, citing de Tocqueville as his authority in his monograph 'The World State, its Organism and Organization', says that he is aware of only two States in the world – Russia and America – which, according to him, enjoy 'absolute sovereignty'. 'Only two centres of power,' he declares, 'Russia and America, can be said to possess untrammelled freedom, and by freedom I mean that they are strong enough technically and politically to assert their absolute primacy among the States.' Jünger goes on to say:

The similarity of the two giants, who can engulf, if not the territories then elements of the sovereignty of the conventional States, almost makes one believe that they are models or, to be more exact, the matrices, the two halves of a mould, by means of which a future world State will one day be shaped. If this were to happen, it would not be a mere addition, a mere duplication, but a transformation of quantity into quality, and the world would scale undreamt-of heights.

And further on he says:

This prospect is attractive above all others because it alone holds out the hope of a restriction and limitation being imposed on the means of power, which have grown too unwieldy for the traditional States and empires to handle. The storage and elimination of these means of power must be the duty of a new central authority, of an 'umbilicus mundi' – a navel of the world. The taming of the still untamed earth fire requires the establishment of a world State. That this will eventually happen can be seen, among other things, from the fact that various ideas of world revolution are robbing the States and their political activities of their former meaning and undermining the concepts of classical war and national frontiers. This is an important change compared with the revolution of 1789 as regards the direct impact produced both on the ethics and the military power of the nation States.

Finally, Jünger arrives at the conclusion – understandable when one bears in mind that he sees events through the eyes of a philosopher – that a linking of the two halves of the 'mould' is not only possible but would result in a change for the better and would in fact lead mankind to the highest and final stage of its evolution. He maintains that he can perceive in his mind's eye that, to all intents and purposes, such a planetary order is already in being, 'with its nature and features already decided'. All that was needed was a formal recognition and proclamation of this truth. 'This could conceivably occur spontaneously – such things have been known to happen – or it could be brought about by virtue of compelling events. At all times, poetry, the poets, must lead the way.'

As we have come to see, however, nothing ever happens merely because it ought to happen. Convincing arguments, based on the compelling power of reason or the splendid visions of philosophers must remain theory. As for the how and when, this is a question that it is beyond our power to answer – a matter either for religious faith or humanist hope. Hence I wish to address myself to the question: What is to be done in the political and military spheres?

For years now we have been going through a 'cold' atomic war fought with varying intensity; at times it has been tough, at others less so. Nor do we have to rely on our imaginations to guess what a 'hot' atomic war would be like, for we have theoretical calculations at our disposal, designed to 'make the unthinkable thinkable'. An American, Professor Seymour Melman, in the summer of 1963 published a study in which, briefly, he forecast the following: The USA at present has an aggregate nuclear arsenal equivalent to 44,000 million tons of TNT, which means that there is 14 tons available for use per head of the world's population. Taking the so-called Hiroshima index as the base, according to which 100,000 dead can be 'produced' with 20,000 tons of TNT, 28 million tons of TNT equivalent would suffice to wipe out completely all major centres of population in the communist-controlled areas of the world. The USSR has a supply of 9,000,000 tons of TNT equivalent for every 100,000 members of the population in the 404 major cities of the NATO area. As for the United States, it has a stock of at least 1,400 million tons for every 100,000 of the population in the 270 major cities of the Soviet bloc. In other

35

words, Washington is in a position to destroy the communist-controlled area 750 times over, while Moscow could, if it so desired destroy the North Atlantic area 450 times over. A further calculation was made by another American, Professor Hermann Kahn. According to his estimate, it would take five years to achieve economic rehabilitation after a war which had cost 10 million dead; the time required would be 20 years if 40 million people had been killed, and 100 years following a war with 160 million fatal casualties.

It is only the realization of these vast dangers which has made the free world see, at long last, what it ought to have seen years ago, i.e. that war has ceased to be a usable instrument in the affairs of nations. A thermo-nuclear weapon of 20 megaton yield – and this is far from being the biggest bomb currently available – would not achieve any rational results. Through its heat flash and blast alone – leaving aside the radioactive devastation which it would cause – it would inflict total destruction over an area of 200 sq. km., heavy damage over an area of 500 sq. km., and partial damage over an area of 2,500 sq. km.

And yet, we cannot be quite sure that this 'Pandora's box' will never be opened. True, the communist world certainly fears nuclear war and is therefore very far from desiring it; it does not, however, consider it an utter impossibility. There is a good deal of evidence to support this contention. In the semi-official Moscow publication 'Military Strategy', prepared in 1963 by Marshal Vasily Danilovich Sokolovsky and eighteen other Red Army generals and colonels, the view is vigorously contested that war has ceased to be a political instrument. 'It is obvious that such views stem from a metaphysical, anti-scientific approach to the social phenomenon of war and are based on an idealization of the new weapons. It is a well-known fact that the nature of war as a continuation of politics by other means does not change with technological evolution.' Sokolovsky goes on to declare *ex cathedra*: 'In terms of its political and social character, the new world war will be the decisive confrontation of the two rival world social systems. This war will inexorably end in victory for the progressive communist social and economic system over the reactionary capitalist system, which is doomed by a law of history to perish.' It is thus evident that the military doctrine of the USSR is a hotchpotch of the eschatological teachings of Karl Marx and the views of Karl von Clausewitz as interpreted by Lenin to suit his own purposes. For the archpriest of the Russian Revolution in March 1918 drew this conclusion from Clausewitz's dictum that war is 'but a continuation of politics by other means': 'Peace is but a breathing space between wars.' Basing himself on this view, a former Chief of the Soviet General Staff, Boris Shaposhnikov, declared that peace must consequently be regarded as but a 'continuation of war by other means'.

What is behind the concept of 'coexistence' – coined by the East – which has so fascinated the West ? Here, too, it would be as well to bear in mind what Sokolovsky has to say in his 'Military Strategy': 'In the present phase the struggle for peace is designed to gain time, above all to enable us resolutely to strengthen the military power of the Soviet Union and the entire socialist camp through the development of their productive forces and the constant expansion of their material and technical foundations.' One is therefore prompted to ask: What situation would the West be faced with if the East were to succeed, during the time thus gained, in achieving a marked military superiority, offering it a real, or apparent, chance of victory ? The theories put forward in communist specialized literature, theories which bristle with bombs and rockets, might easily become a deadly reality in that event!

It may well be that it is now out of the question for anyone to gain a military victory in a contest fought out in the traditional three elements, however large the theatre of war. This is evidently one of the reasons for the present bid to turn the so-called 'cosmic flank' of the prospective enemy. In the autumn of 1914, after the Battle of the Marne, the German and Anglo-French armies again and again tried to outflank one another until they finally reached the Atlantic. Now, half a century later, there is a race in progress between the USA and the Soviet Union to decide which will turn the other's 'cosmic flank', in accordance with the dictum of Archimedes: 'Give me a point outside the earth where I can stand and I shall lift the earth off its hinges.' Who will lift the earth off its hinges ? Mankind has had to live with this nightmarish question for a long time now, and the problem will continue to prey on our minds even if the non-proliferation treaty does come into force universally.

The power of deterrence, which was a credible proposition so long as the United States had a nuclear monopoly and was in a position to threaten a massive retaliatory blow in the event of a Soviet decision to commit aggression against America or Europe, began to lose some of its impact with the development of Russian nuclear weapons. Once Washington had come within the range of Moscow's bombers and long-range missiles, a credible nuclear guarantee by the New World to the Old could no longer be counted on with absolute certainty.

General Maxwell D. Taylor was the first to describe the results of this development.* He began his review of the situation by pointing out that there were limits upon the possibilities of the USA's power of nuclear retaliation. Having regard to the circumstances likely to obtain during the few years to come, Taylor considered that neither the Americans nor their allies and enemies believed that the USA was really prepared to use its power of retaliation for any purpose other than self-preservation. What were the circumstances in which the country's very existence would be in danger? This would be the case in two clearly defined contingencies: a nuclear attack on the American mainland, or the discovery of incontrovertible evidence that such an attack was about to be launched. A third possibility would be a large-scale attack on Western Europe, since the loss of this area to communism would ultimately endanger American national existence. These, then, were the only circumstances that could be envisaged in which the Americans could justify the deliberate use of their power to strike a retaliatory blow. These were the only contingencies in which the power of deterrence would come into the reckoning.

The idea of a 'limited war' began to arouse interest once Taylor had mooted it as one way to deal with the new situation. He maintained that the US Government's programme for a strategy of flexible response should from the outset renounce the concept of massive retaliation. It should be made clear that the USA is getting ready to strike back, wherever and whenever necessary, with such weapons and troops as might best meet the needs of the situation in hand. In so doing, Taylor believed, the Americans could restore to warfare its historic justification of being the means

*The Uncertain Trumpet, 1959

whereby a better world could be created once hostilities had been successfully concluded.

Not only did this appear to be a solution to our current problems but it seemed to open up once again the possibility of rational warfare. The idea set off an avalanche of pamphlets, analyses and theories; in the United States alone no fewer than 328 works were published in this context in the period up to 1966. However, experience teaches us to be sceptical. The notion that common sense can be maintained in wartime is, when all is said and done, only comparatively recent, since it dates back to the Age of Reason. As long ago as 1933, Guglielmo Ferrero noted in his book *Peace and War*: 'Limited warfare was one of the finest flowers of the eighteenth century. It is a kind of hothouse plant which can only thrive in an aristocratic civilization based on noble values. We are no longer suited to it. It is one of the excellent things we have lost as a result of the French Revolution.'

Admittedly, recourse to 'limited war' would be a logical, rational move. But unfortunately, such a solution leaves out of account the laws of psychology, which is concerned with emotional processes. To believe that one might, if need be, draw the conventional dagger so as to be able to leave the nuclear sword in its sheath, would be to risk overlooking the dangers which would be bound to result from such a course. The fact is – once we stop worrying about the consequences of a nuclear catastrophe, we shall be tempted to think of the use of conventional weapons as something that can be justified. This would actually favour the outbreak of war. And war, though it would begin with conventional weapons, might nevertheless finish up as a nuclear inferno, and in fact this may well be inevitable. The truth is that it is hardly possible to put a brake on the escalation of anger once a life-and-death struggle has begun. It must be assumed that in such a situation an escalation in the use of weapons would follow automatically. The war would therefore grow worse and worse step by step, and having started with a non-nuclear stage, it would then reach a stage entailing the use of tactical nuclear weapons; finally, total horror would ensue with an exchange of nuclear blows by the two giants. The fact is that the vanquished side in a conventional war would either have to obey the 'rules of the game' and admit defeat or resort to the use of more effective weapons. In the latter case, it would be faced with the very dilemma it had hoped to avoid in choosing to fight a limited war with conventional weapons. And it would have to confront this situation in a worse plight since, by renouncing the use of the nuclear threat, it would have courted war and defeat and would now have to seek to extricate itself from this predicament at the risk of suicide by employing nuclear weapons. Warfare is not a game of chess with set rules, for it may well happen that the contestant who has been losing his chessmen on the board of conventional warfare may suddenly get up from his chair and hit his adversary square in the face in order to put him out of action.

Some people may object that all military conflicts which occurred since 1945 have been fought out as 'limited wars'. And it is an undeniable fact that conventional weapons only were used in the 43 confrontations that took place in the last twenty years in which shots were actually exchanged. Of these conflicts, 26 must be regarded as civil wars and 17 as wars between States; all of them, however, took place in peripheral areas. None of the nuclear Powers saw its interests threatened to such an extent as to feel itself obliged to engage in a life-and-death struggle. Apart from conflicts which must be regarded as merely the bloody outcome of the chaos produced by anti-colonialism, all we have seen – considered in historical terms – has been mutual sparring by the real adversaries. Admittedly, in Korea, this cost a million human lives. The East was looking for soft spots in the West's armour, while the West was trying to contain the East's aggression.

In a mood compounded of helplessness and fear, the West has been indulging in intellectual self-deception. For some considerable time now it has regarded the East as not necessarily an adversary but a competitor. The error inherent in this appraisal was analysed by Wilhelm Cornides in his contribution to the anthology 'Strategy of Disarmament'. He notes:

Within any economic system, whatever it may be, two competing concerns can vie with one another for the biggest share of the market while at the same time making the occasional deal about the price and quality of their goods. However, hostility is not the same as competition – it is a conflict. Whether States are 'competing' or in 'conflict' with one another depends not only on their power structure but also on the quality of their mutual recognition or otherwise, i.e. it depends on whether they are prepared to accept their respective frontiers and their continued existence within those frontiers as part of the international order, and also on whether that order is itself a bone of contention.

However, the nature of the East-West confrontation is such that the two systems – the liberal-democratic system of the West and the totalitarian communist system of the East – cannot accept one another without at the same time renouncing the very basis of their existence. We are thus in the presence, not of competition but of a struggle, a conflict. The mistaken assumption – due to autosuggestion – that this is not the case has again and again induced the West to try for an understanding with the East, upon which – so it is believed – it would be possible to base a stable edifice of common interests. The fact that the morality of the free world differs in essence from that of the so-called socialist camp is usually overlooked in this connection. Lenin, whose doctrines remain binding upon communists, was a spiritual successor to Niccolo Machiavelli. Lenin's address to the Third All-Russian Congress of the Young Communist League in 1920 strikes one as being wholly in line with Machiavelli's thought. Lenin declared: 'We reject any morality which is derived from supernatural, classless concepts. We declare such concepts to be a deceit, a swindle intended to befuddle the minds of the workers and peasants in the interest of the landowners and capitalists. We declare our morality to be wholly subordinated to the interests of the proletarian class struggle. We derive our morality from the interests of the proletarian class struggle.'

Since the East's challenge to the West has not been withdrawn and since common ethical standards can hardly be said to exist between the two camps, the struggle – despite occasional phases of relaxation – is bound to go on. Minor shooting wars are scarcely likely to alter the situation to any marked extent. Even the old-style peripheral military clashes have not produced – nor can they produce – decisions likely to endure. For the giants who are involved in these confrontations have all along seen the danger that they might quickly be faced with the nuclear challenge they are so anxious to avoid. The armed conflict in Korea ended with its original cause – the country's division – being revived. And in Vietnam the Americans are merely fighting for the restoration of the status quo ante – for a sham peace based on the division of that country. The upshot of the clash in Cuba was the same unsatisfactory result that can be expected in Vietnam: The outcome of the confrontation in the Caribbean, with the forces of the two sides being put on a war footing, was by no means an American victory. True, the USSR had to withdraw its rockets from the island, but in return Moscow received a guarantee that Washington would allow Havana to go unscathed; consequently, the problem remained unsolved.

Attempts are being made, by closing the membership list of the nuclear club, to prevent the 'fall from grace' which would result in the forces of hell being let loose. But all the time the number of unresolved problems is rising, more and more explosive matter is being allowed to accumulate in the world and the danger is growing of a world conflagration, liable to result from a number of smaller explosions and to affect countries in no way originally involved.

How can we escape from this dilemma? A French general, André Beaufre, put forward a fascinating argument in his book 'Total Art of War in Peace'. He states that the advent of the atomic bomb has 'at one and the same time made both large-scale war and genuine peace a thing of the past'. He notes in particular:

The developments of the last ten years have shown up the fatal errors which have been committed because people have tried to deal with these problems empirically, by rule of thumb, against adversaries who know the game inside out. We must learn to play the game with the same realism and cold logic in order to prevent our general position from becoming progressively eroded. We must also avoid a situation arising where a desperate step might become necessary, a step which, in present-day conditions and because of the mechanism of direct strategy, would render a catastrophe inevitable. We must learn to survive in 'peace' and to save such remnants of peace as can still be saved. We must master the art of indirect strategy.

But, of course, the East finds it easier than the West to develop ways of applying an indirect 'cold' strategy. The British author John Fuller has noted in this context that the fundamental difference between the policy of the democracies and that of the Soviet Union is due to their respective concepts of the nature of peace. While in the eyes of the democrats peace begins where war leaves off, for the Soviets peace is merely a continuation of war, all the means of combat being used. While in the democratic view international disputes are in time of peace to be settled by negotiation, for the Soviets such negotiations are a means of sharpening the conflict. In the democracies government is based on collective decisions, the ballot box and public opinion; in the Soviet Union, on the other hand, it rests on the authority of a single man or a small ruling clique, i.e. on the decision of a handful of individuals. It follows from this that it is easy for the Soviets to maintain a permanent state of war, with the leaders playing the decisive role and with the policies adopted being virtually uninfluenced by public opinion and secrecy securely maintained. In the democratic countries, on the other hand, none of this is possible except in wartime. Like a mob which is confronted with the might of disciplined troops, the democrats withdraw in the face of Soviet power, frightened to exploit the Soviets' difficulties.

There are historical parallels for such a situation. The actions of the free world recall those of the democratic Athenians when confronted by Philip of Macedonia. It was in vain that Demosthenes called on them:

When you hear that Philip is in the Chersonese, you vote in favour of a campaign in the Chersonese; when he appears at Thermopylae, you cast your vote in favour of a campaign there. Wherever he is, you follow him step by step, moving hither and thither all the time. You take your marching orders from him. Never do you plan a campaign yourselves; never do you foresee an event until you are told that something has happened or has been happening. ... It is not our business to guess what the future may bring; we may be sure that it will bring us misfortune if you do not look the facts in the face. ...

In other words, the *pax atomica*, reflected in the dualism of the two super-powers, in no way automatically safeguards peace. On the contrary, it demands – to use Beaufre's phrase – the application of the 'total art of war in peace', an art which the East has so far evidently mastered more effectively than the West. In view of this, it is nothing short of touching to see how NATO has been evolving its military doctrine under the influence of the American planners of strategy, the US 'desk warriors'. In the past, it used to be the custom to assess the extent of a military threat according to the potential of the prospective enemy. The latter was always credited with a potential superior to his actual strength at any given time. Hence the two hundred Soviet divisions, whose appearance in the European theatre of war would, it was believed, swiftly follow the outbreak of hostilities. But from 1961 onwards this potential was assessed at a lower level; the total of Soviet divisions was reduced – perhaps because it had originally been overestimated but perhaps also because a lower estimate of Soviet divisions, say ninety – made it easier to renounce massive deterrence and to accept the doctrine of a 'limited war' fought with conventional weapons. Finally, the practice was adopted of downgrading the military threat not only in quantitative but also in qualitative terms, on the basis of an evaluation, not of the prospective enemy's potential but of a theoretical analysis of his intentions.

If one's aim is to evolve a strategy based on the 'art of war in peace' which is undoubtedly necessary – one must have adequate power. Where an individual State lacks such power, it must seek to attain it in association with other States whose strategic interests are largely in accord with its own. This in itself justifies the call for the political unification of Europe, since America can be relied upon only conditionally to align her concepts with Europe's requirements, and these can only be partially identical with those of the USA.

# *Relaxation of Tension among the Great Powers*

What sort of picture does the West now present to the political observer? We can see the North Atlantic Pact, which was at one time regarded by many as an unbreakable union for better or worse degenerating into a coalition of the traditional type, into a sort of 'company with limited liability'. Its partners still feel that they are linked by certain ties, but no longer for good or ill. The Pact has more or less turned into a series of bilateral military alliances, with the USA acting in each case as one partner and country 'X' as the other.

The hope that we should see an 'Atlantic Union' evolve stage by stage – possibly a confederation of States – has been disappointed and has turned out to be a piece of pious self-deception, a beautiful illusion which had been fostered by the assumption that the allied nations would, inspired by their common ideals, forget about their divergent interests. Another reason for the failure was the mistaken belief of a number of leading Americans who thought that partnership with the United States was more important than European unity. They were losing sight of the fact that Europe's unity is a precondition for the establishment of strong transatlantic ties. George Ball considers this type of thinking 'thoroughly wrongheaded'. According to him,

. . . Until Europe knows the reality of roughly equivalent power, Europeans will never risk the full acceptance of a partnership relation. They are quite aware that a junior partner has little to say about the affairs of a firm, and unless they feel equal in fact they will be likely to regard 'partnership' as a Yankee device designed to induce them to serve as bush-beaters and gun-bearers in support of United States policies – including policies of which they are skeptical and in the making of which they have had little voice. . . .

. . . I am convinced, therefore, that there can be no truly easy and effective partnership between America and Europe until there is a Europe in the political sense.

But the determination of the allies to meet any danger threatening them all by joint action did not in itself prove enough to overcome their traditional differences. Those differences had only been temporarily shelved under the impact of Eastern pressure, and their virulence revived as soon as the pressure on the West seemed to be subsiding and 'relaxation' was beginning to make itself felt.

The erosion of NATO, which everybody deplores, is thus not the cause, but the consequence, of the fact that it had proved impossible to co-ordinate permanently the efforts of the various partners to the Pact, that it had proved impossible to make the partners march in unison in response to the simple command 'one for all and all for one'. The various States which together make up the alliance look upon themselves as historic entities. They are not ready, or not yet ready, to become part of a bigger unit and to subordinate their individual requirements to the needs of the whole. This may be deplored and regarded as outdated, but the facts are as they are and will have to be taken into account as a permanent source of controversy among the North Atlantic partners. It is these facts which are bound to determine the future shape of the alliance. There is no point in closing one's eyes to experience, in trying to behave as if the facts were not what they are. We must no longer blind ourselves to the fact that the effectiveness of the Western community will be reduced to the extent to which each of its members pleads the principle of *ultra posse nemo obligatur*. In this connection, the objective differences between America's interests and those of Europe, as well as the subjective variations in the various partners' assessment of the dangers threatening and the specific tasks to be performed are bound to be of crucial importance, with *sacro egoismo* frequently being hidden under a cloak of selfless devotion to the welfare of the world.

'As sovereign States, the partners to the alliance are under no obligation to subordinate their policies to collective decisions.'

This is the literal text, word for word, of a document entitled 'The Future Tasks of the Alliance', adopted by the NATO Council of Ministers on 14 December 1967.

'Where are the good old days of NATO', plaintively asked the *Washington Post* – a liberal paper which tends to reflect more accurately than any of its contemporaries the views of the Democratic Administration – in the summer of 1967. 'With the relaxation of East-West tension,' said the paper, 'the free world had lost its *esprit de corps* to a frightening degree.' The paper's gloomy view closely reflected feelings which one tends to encounter more and more frequently in meetings with American politicians, officials and officers on either side of the Atlantic. And no one can, in fact, deny the justice of the American complaints that France is working strenuously for the disintegration of the alliance, that Britain is steadily diminishing its contribution to it, and that not even from the Federal Republic is the alliance receiving as much support as its senior commanders at one time thought themselves entitled to expect. . . .

Though one cannot deny the justice of the USA's criticisms of its partners in the alliance, one is nevertheless amazed at the failure of the Americans so far to grasp the fact that it is they themselves who have started this process of erosion of the Pact and that it is thus not only the French, the British and the Germans who must be considered responsible. It would be to confuse cause and effect to blame this evil on Europe's weariness of the alliance while completely overlooking the fact that this reaction is largely a reflex occasioned by America's attitude. The 'good old days of NATO', whose passing everyone deplores, date back to a time when US strategy still provided an entirely credible defence against Soviet pressures and threats, a time when the leading Power's hegemony was based on its unchallenged position of patronage over those under its protection.

During the fifties, the underlying concept of the alliance rested on the assumption that the Europeans would provide a 'shield' in the form of conventional forces (equipped also, from 1958 onwards, with tactical nuclear weapons) while the Americans would discharge the task of deterrence, using their nuclear arsenal as the alliance's 'sword'. This disposition – aimed at first at massive retaliation and later at providing a graduated response – seemed,

47

as far as was humanly foreseeable, to have made war impossible, so that it afforded complete cover for all the security interests of the allies. However, the emergence of the 'nuclear stalemate' of the two giants – the USA and the USSR – transformed the situation during the early sixties. Under the presidency of John F. Kennedy, American strategy in Europe was 'renationalized', which resulted in a reversal of this policy. According to a statement made by Defence Secretary McNamara in December 1962, the means of mass destruction were henceforth to be regarded as the 'shield' and the conventional forces as the 'sword'. In practical terms, this meant that a brake was being put on the policy of deterrence in Europe, entirely in accordance with the views of General Taylor, referred to in the previous chapter.

This might in part be explained by the fact that Washington now believed itself more secure than ever before. Moreover, there appeared to be an intention to stabilize the 'nuclear stalemate' – the 'balance of terror' as between Washington and Moscow – at the level then obtaining. The effect of the 'nuclear balance' between the two giants now rests solely on the fact that both the Russians and the Americans are in possession of adequate 'second strike capability', both in terms of quantity and quality, with the result that their arsenal of intercontinental missiles is safe from a 'first strike' by the enemy. They are therefore in a position to retaliate against an attack on their own territory with a 'second strike' against that of the enemy. It follows from this that each of the two super-powers now has its finger not only on its own 'nuclear trigger' but in effect also on that of the other side; neither dare fire the first shot since, by so doing, it would automatically trigger off the second round, by which it would itself be hit. Since any decision to kill the enemy now virtually amounts to suicide, a position of mutual paralysis has emerged as between the USSR and the USA. Although this situation owes its existence to mutual fear, it nevertheless provides the two countries with security from attack by one another.

Seeing that the balance of power has produced such useful results, Washington has based its strategy on it and has sought to persuade Moscow to follow suit. There seemed to be a basis for the application of the concept of 'arms control', for a rational armaments policy aimed at preserving the second strike capability of both sides. This concept presupposed that both sides would deliberately renounce any attempt at creating a situation in which a 'first strike' might again become a tempting proposition.

These, then, are the aims which America – despite some contrary trends – is trying to achieve in Europe: She wants to see a 'bipolar security system' established in Europe, which would be based on guarantees furnished by both Washington and Moscow. This, in turn, presupposes a consolidation of the status quo, and would seem to call for an agreement, at least de facto, guaranteeing the present territorial arrangements. In other words, the mutual relationship in our continent of the two World Powers is gradually to be 'normalized', passing from a stage of competing coexistence to co-operation and finally to the establishment of a condominium.

This, admittedly, is only a rough outline – possibly too rough – of America's blueprint for Europe's future. My sketch may lack the softer touches of light and shade, but anyone who cares to examine it soberly is bound to see why Washington no longer considers it to be NATO's chief role to 'deter' but mainly to provide an instrument for 'arms control'. The idea is to induce Moscow to cease regarding the alliance as a threat. On the contrary, the USSR is to look upon NATO as an instrument for the supervision of its members, especially the Federal Republic. During the last few years the USA has endeavoured with angelic patience to explain this to the USSR, without, however, meeting with much understanding. For the present, at any rate, the Russians are evidently not prepared to make their Warsaw Pact fit in with the Americans' ideas about a 'reform' of NATO. This would seem to bear out the contention of the Italian writer Ignazio Silone: 'International negotiations are so difficult because the arguments have to be translated not only from one language into another but from one ideology into another.'

America blames the difficulties which she is encountering in connection with her efforts to achieve a relaxation of tension – efforts which, as I have explained, are based on exceedingly complex concepts – on Moscow's suspicions. She knows that East-West understandings relying on a spirit of 'give and take' are out of reach for the time being. Hence the notion that 'good examples' – one might call them carefully graduated advance concessions – will by and by allow trust to grow in the Soviet Union. Hence, no doubt, also the reduction in US troop levels in Germany. This measure is thus not to be regarded as merely a consequence of the Vietnam war or of the worsening of the American balance of payments; it must be considered a US 'signal' to the USSR, a hint that the USA is ready to join in a gradual disengagement and progressive denuclearization.

Adelbert Weinstein, who can scarcely be accused of viewing US policy with morbid suspicion, commented in the *Frankfurter Allgemeine Zeitung* of 3 May 1967:

The intended withdrawal of four US Air Force units from the Federal Republic is bound to make one think. We can understand many of the worries which are on our partners' minds, and though we cannot approve the transfer of some thirty thousand American Army personnel back to the States, we can see the reasons for it. However, as for the reduction of allied air strength, we cannot view this with the same equanimity. There is more involved here than mere desire to save money. The withdrawal of American aircraft has nothing to do with fiscal considerations. A change in strategic thinking is clearly emerging. Modern high-performance aircraft are equipped with nuclear weapons, or at least they can be fitted for a nuclear mission in a matter of hours. By transferring military aircraft, the Americans have started a process which must lead to a weakening of Europe's nuclear front. No one doubts that the West still retains an 'overkill' capacity. The nuclear superiority of the Americans – and hence that of their allies – remains crushing. But from the fact that the emphasis in nuclear policy has been shifted from Europe to America it can be deduced that, so far as the security policy of the Atlantic alliance is concerned, a process of denuclearization has been set in motion. It must be assumed that matters will not be allowed to rest there, for strategic policies follow their own logic. The policy of deterrence by permanent threat is now being abandoned in favour of a policy aimed at maintaining peace through a sort of understanding among accomplices – in this case the two nuclear giants.

True, Washington is encountering a whole series of major obstacles – above all in Berlin – in its endeavour to change NATO into an instrument for 'arms control'. Secretary of State Dean Rusk, who tends to analyse developments more subtly than his colleague, Defence Secretary McNamara, made this very clear in a statement during a congressional committee hearing. If that isolated city, that 'hostage to fortune', did not exist, he said, the 'problems of the East-West confrontation', and an agreement on arrangements within NATO, would be much easier. The measures taken by the Pankow Government against free access to Berlin are certain to have been agreed with, and approved by, Moscow in advance. This shows clearly what the rulers in Pankow – who both aid Moscow and egg it on – think of the solidity of the Atlantic alliance now that its underlying concepts are being called into question.

What Rusk meant by his statement becomes clear when one realizes that the Western enclave in the East remains secure only so long as deterrence remains effective. To dismantle the apparatus designed to keep it effective would be to run the risk that one day the Russians might gain possession of this outpost of freedom in order to use it as a hostage. If this were to happen, the Americans, who have invested the whole of their prestige in Berlin, would find their position as the world's greatest Power directly threatened. We can only hope that they are aware of this, and it is up to us Germans to remember what an asset America's obligations in connection with our former capital are to the security of the Federal Republic.

The ambivalence of American policy – its fluctuations from deterrence to 'relaxation' – facilitated agreement on the minimum compromise regarding NATO's strategy which was adopted at the Brussels Conference on 12 December 1967. The NATO Committee for Defence Planning – the so-called Group of Fourteen, i.e. the NATO allies minus France – added to the political directives adopted at the last Paris meeting on 9 May 1967 a military programme which provides for a three-stage strategy of defence against aggression in Europe. During the first stage, an attempt is to be made to try and hold up the enemy's onslaught by means of 'direct defence' – mainly by using conventional forces. Should this fail, the second stage – that of 'deliberate escalation' – would follow. This phase, we are authoritatively told, will consist of the use of nuclear weapons for 'selective strikes' against enemy troops and targets within tactical range behind the enemy front. Should none of this produce the desired effect, the 'ultimate means' will be resorted to, a generalized exchange of nuclear strikes between America and Russia. These three stages –

so Document MC 14/3 declares – will not be treated as strictly separate in terms of time and space, so that each stage will have some of the characteristics of the other two.

Compared with the original draft produced by the Military Committee – which called for a battle for the destiny of our continent fought by conventional means 'to the bitter end' – the policy just described must be considered a welcome change, an improvement making for a more sophisticated use of the deterrent, with its effect resting on the impossibility of calculating in advance the risks involved in an attack. Nevertheless, it would be a mistake to ignore the fact that there are trends growing within NATO which favour the use of 'crisis management' even after the outbreak of hostilities, as well as 'controlled warfare' à la Vietnam. It is becoming increasingly clear that these tactics of 'no victory' tend to produce results which are actually worse than mere failure to win victory.

The new strategy of 'flexible response' is the same in name only as the old doctrine known by that designation, since the West's potential is no longer sufficient to ensure that every type of attack is met with an adequate response. France has dropped out as a logistic base and source of troops. The United States has to date removed thirty-five thousand troops from Germany, and it must be doubted whether the transport of troops by sea and air could fill the gap in an emergency. It is to be expected, moreover, that the personnel rotation system of the US armed services will in future involve even larger numbers of troops. As for Britain, she has withdrawn six thousand men as part of her 'redeployment'. Belgium is to reduce her contribution to NATO by some twelve thousand troops, two of her six brigades having been disbanded.

Having regard to the implications of this entire process, it would be logical to lower the 'nuclear threshold' somewhat. However, the USA – for understandable reasons which are to do with its national security dispositions – would like to raise this threshold. As a result, a gap has been created between the aims and the capabilities of the alliance, a gap which cannot be filled by military means and which has only been partially filled politically – to the extent to which the Pact has the backing of a Washington guarantee. Although McNamara indicated on 9 May 1967 that his country no longer intended to tie itself to a definite long-term strategy,

Paul Nitze, on 12 December 1967 renewed US assurances that America continues to give priority to the defence of Europe despite her involvement in Asia. We must believe these assurances and are in fact behaving accordingly, chiefly because to do otherwise would do us more harm than good.

Nevertheless, the question must be asked: How much longer will this foundation remain capable of bearing the weight of the Pact? How much longer are we entitled to expect the Americans to pull the Europeans' chestnuts out of the fire in an emergency? How long before the USA, which is coming to feel that it is being challenged to a nuclear arms race by its adversary in world affairs, becomes tired of its allies, who because of their lack of solidarity, are incapable of looking after their own security?

If one could safely assume that the present comparative calm in our continent will continue and that the dangers inherent in the presence, side by side, of two opposed systems of government are not likely to become acute, the present tactics of muddling along could possibly be justified. However, it must be feared that any efforts aimed at creating a stable order – whatever its exact shape – in our part of the world are bound, in the last resort, to fail. In any case, why should the East be prepared to make that minimum of concessions which we are bound to demand since it can see that the West is busily engaged in undermining the foundations of its own security? The NATO Council of Ministers was absolutely right in declaring that, far from there being a contradiction between military strength and political relaxation, these two aims are complementary. However, such fine words cut very little ice in a situation where the deeds are in stark contrast to the words.

And is it indeed true that Soviet policy is really as anxious to secure a 'relaxation' at present, as some would have us believe? Moscow is having considerable difficulties with several Warsaw Pact States. In view of this, is it really only concerned with consolidating its position in Europe? Is the Kremlin really as eager as all that to show the world a friendly face? Are we justified in hoping that the seventies will prove to be a decade of peace in our continent and especially in Germany?

A number of people have lately been spreading rumours that the Russians are secretly 'thinning out' their troops in Central

Germany,* thus following the 'good example' set by the Anglo-Saxon Powers in Western Germany. The Soviets, we are told, have kept quiet about this move so as not to frighten their comrades in Pankow. Unfortunately, this theory, which appears to hint at the possibility of a 'creeping disengagement' on the other side of the demarcation line, is based on wishful thinking. When all is said and done, why should the USSR wish to reduce its troop strength between the Elbe and the Oder in secret? Moreover, are we seriously expected to believe that the Pankow authorities have failed to notice that thousands of Red Army troops have been secretly withdrawn?

The fact is that any diminution of the military potential which the USSR maintains in the centre of our continent would be totally inconsistent with the realities of the situation. In Russia, the propaganda machine is working all out to emphasize the so-called 'threat of war', which has supposedly been created by a 'conspiracy' between the 'imperialists', 'revanchists' and 'zionists'. To mark the fiftieth anniversary of the communist October Revolution, the 'Theses' of the Communist Party of the Soviet Union were distributed throughout the USSR. Long-winded and dull though this document may be, it shows very clearly how far the party which rules the USSR has lately abandoned the policy of 'liberalization'. While liberalizing tendencies are emerging in the other countries of the eastern bloc, the Kremlin rulers are reverting to their former tough line. The leading role of the Party is again being strongly emphasized and Marxist-Leninist indoctrination is being strengthened. Writers are being imprisoned, theatre plays critical of the regime cancelled, Western diplomats shadowed and contacts between Soviet citizens and foreigners more closely supervised and made more difficult if not altogether impossible. Apartment blocks for foreigners in Moscow have been fenced in and put under police surveillance, children of foreigners are being kept apart from Russian children and taught in special schools.

The orthodox dogmatism and militant tone of the Theses belies the image of the Soviet Union as a peace-loving World Power which is so often projected in the West. Even though the Theses do not officially proclaim the need for a 're-Stalinization',

*I.e. East Germany – .

the fact that numerous theories which date back to the Stalin era are now being revived in effect amounts to just that. It may be that much of the propaganda which is being drummed into the people is the work of obtuse, overzealous Party ideologists, the fact still remains that the pamphlet as a whole is typical of the reactionary tendencies which inspire the present Soviet leaders.

The historical review which takes up a great deal of space in the Theses is in effect an apologia for Stalin. The Caucasian dictator comes in for only one reproach – his cult of personality – while his actions are praised fulsomely. Surprisingly, the Theses even justify his 1939 pact with Hitler. It is claimed that the pact foiled the 'plans of the imperialists', gained time for the USSR to rearm and made possible its 'reunification' with Moldavia, the Ukraine, Byelorussia and the Baltic States. The failure to gauge Hitler's war plans correctly is blamed entirely on the Army leaders, while Stalin is credited with having won a glorious victory. As for the efforts of the allies, they are clearly considered to have been of no importance since the Soviet historians do not mention them by so much as a single word.

In these foreign policy Theses, the Soviet leaders define their attitude vis-à-vis both China and America. The policy of the 'Mao Tse-tung clique' comes in for strong condemnation and is compared with the attitude of Trotsky. At the same time, the Theses express the hope that the Chinese Party will abandon Mao's policy and rebuild China's former relations with the USSR. One reason why this is necessary, according to the Theses, is that thanks to America there is a danger of a third world war. According to the Moscow document, it is Washington which is responsible for the Vietnam war, for 'Israel's insolent attack on the Arabs, the 'constant provocations against Cuba', the 'fascist regime in Greece' and 'West German revanchism'. All these allegations strongly recall Stalin's theory of 'imperialist encirclement'.

'Coexistence' is mentioned in the Theses only incidentally. On the other hand, there is a great deal of talk in the document about the theory of 'just wars', and it is claimed in this connection that the USSR accords its support exclusively to 'wars for the defence of the peoples' gains in the struggle against imperialist aggression, to wars for national liberation and wars waged by revolutionary classes against the forces of reaction'. According to the document, the USSR's outstanding achievement in the last fifty years is its success in securing an 'all-round increase in its defensive strength'. The aim of Soviet policy is said to be a shift in the balance of power in the world to the detriment of 'imperialism' and in favour of the 'triumph of the communist revolution on a world scale' by ensuring the uninterrupted growth of the USSR's economic and military power. There are no statements on disarmament or initiatives for peace in the Theses, such as were issued in connection with the twentieth Congress of the CPSU.

The Soviet marshals and admirals showed off the might of their weapons to mark the fiftieth anniversary of the Soviet armed forces with an ostentation that recalled their counterparts in Kaiser Wilhelm's Germany. But despite this, it is most unlikely that any of the leaders of the Soviet bloc expects a clash of arms with the West to occur in the immediate future. Their sabre rattling is designed to justify their arms expenditure on the grounds that it is necessary for defence.

What other reason could there possibly be for the various States of the Warsaw Pact to increase their military budgets one after another in what can only be described as a deliberate demonstration? The Soviet Union started this process; the so-called 'German Democratic Republic' promptly followed suit, and Poland and Hungary then did likewise. . . . There can be no doubt that this is a policy which contrasts strikingly with present trends and plans in the West.

Admittedly, the Eastern military budgets seem relatively modest when compared with their Western equivalents. Moscow's military expenditure in 1968 (at the official rate of exchange) amounted to £7,400 million; the East Berlin regime's to £580 million; Poland's to £480 million and Hungary's to £210 million. Having regard to the size of the armed forces of these countries, these are ridiculously small sums. Russia has 3,800,000 men under arms; the. Soviet zone* 210,000; Poland 350,000 and Hungary 140,000. Since these armies do not live on air and since their up-to-date arms and other equipment are far from cheap, it is obvious that the budget figures are false. Totalitarian regimes, which are not subject to the control of free parliaments, consider themselves

*I.e. East Germany – .

to be under no obligation to furnish accurate and true figures regarding their arms expenditure. Much of this expenditure – something like thirty to sixty per cent according to one estimate – is camouflaged and included in other budget appropriations.

This practice of hiding the true expenditure, customary in the communist countries, greatly detracts from the value of their official military budget figures. Regardless of whether these figures show a rise or a fall, they do not provide any hard and fast evidence on which the democratic world could possibly base an assessment of the situation. This being the case, we must be all the more careful to look upon the size of the defence budgets announced by the East as signals designed to serve political and psychological ends.

Moscow has been getting ready to adopt a 'global strategy', i.e. it has been equipping its military machine to operate on 'external', instead of, as hitherto, exclusively along 'internal' lines. In other words, the aim is to ensure that the Soviet forces can put in an appearance at any important point of the globe at any time. Yugoslav commentators, who have long since ceased to regard their 'big brother' with hostility, have noted that the Soviet Union's strategic doctrine, which traditionally used to emphasize the defensive role of the Soviet forces, is now changing and giving priority to the offensive. This does not necessarily mean that the USSR is setting a course for direct aggression; what it does mean is that the USSR will henceforth appear on the scene more frequently to provide military cover for its 'clients' in any crisis which it may have instigated and nourished by political means.

In his last report – issued one month before leaving office – US Defence Secretary McNamara had to admit that during the year 1967 the USSR was able to raise the total of its land-based intercontinental ballistic missiles from 340 to 720. In other words, the Soviet Union is getting pretty close to achieving the level of deterrence possessed by the USA, which itself has 1,054 ICBMs. It is only in regard to sea-borne missiles, installed in submarines, that the USA is still markedly superior to the USSR, their respective totals of such missiles being 656 and 30. In this connection, it may be as well to recall that in medium-range missiles, such as now threaten Europe, the Russians have for years been superior to the Americans – the figures in this area at present being 750 to 0 in favour of the Russians.

Developments in the sphere of rocket armaments – e.g. anti-missile missiles, multiple warheads and orbital weapons – seem to indicate that the 'second strike strategy', the peace-saving function of the 'nuclear stalemate', is now in some danger. A number of experts have pointed this out, in Germany notably Wolfram von Raven:

> Those who take their cue from the facts and not from wishful thinking will have to agree that the Soviets have never really co-operated with the Americans in their 'arms control' policy, despite the fact that this policy implied an offer of coexistence based on constructive co-operation and even on a condominium. They merely made use of it because they saw in it a chance of achieving 'parity' with, and eventually 'superiority' over, the Americans.

To this one might add: Apart from anything else, it has always been the Russians' aim in this connection to eliminate the German Federal Republic as a political and military factor and to reduce the chances of a West European coalition being established.

Thomas Wolfe of the Rand Corporation of Santa Monica, California, during a series of US Senate hearings which took place towards the end of 1967, presented a comprehensive analysis in which he sought to define Moscow's aims in the contest with Washington. He dismissed the first theoretical contingency as 'improbable in practice'. This was that the USSR, believing that it had a chance of victory, might launch a large-scale attack on the USA. But he thought this impossible in view of the nature of the present collective leadership in the Kremlin and its philosophy of 'Marxist determinism'. The second contingency – i.e. that the Soviet Union, believing itself secure in the present status quo – might accept a US proposal that this status be maintained and that it would therefore help to consolidate the peace, was also inconceivable. Only the third possibility was described by Wolfe as realistic. It is, according to him, that the Russians may begin to revive old, unsolved, 'latent' issues and combine this with thrusts into the 'third world'.

It is a fact that behind the 'safety barrier' provided by the strategic weapons, which is constantly being raised and strengthened, developments are taking place in conventional arms technology which would seem to support this view. The Soviets are trying to emulate the Americans in a bid to achieve global mobility. This is evident both from their efforts to force the pace of naval rearmament and from the fact that they have considerably expanded and improved their air transport capability. Moscow wishes to become strong enough to challenge Washington at any point on earth. In the Mediterranean – which Europeans think ought to be their *mare nostro* – the Americans have acquired irksome companions who are trying to shadow their Sixth Fleet. It follows that in the event of a Middle East war, direct involvement of the Great Powers would be a distinct possibility.

The Russian bear has long since learnt how to swim and now evidently feels that the time has come for him to relinquish his former defensive strategy, which was one of coastal defence in depth, and to become active in distant waters. The Soviet Navy is being expanded by the addition of major long-range units, and is also being improved in terms of quality. Its vessels are being equipped with guided missiles of the 'Styx' type, which accounted for the Israeli destroyer Eilath in 1967. Moreover, an aircraft carrier is now in course of construction, of which it is not yet known whether it will be able to accommodate bombers – perhaps of the VTOL type – or only helicopters.

In addition, the USSR is building up a potential for combined operations. The number of landing craft is being increased and a Marine force set up. At the moment, the total of Red 'leathernecks' has only reached 7,500 – insufficient for an expeditionary corps – but enough to form the nucleus of such a force. To mount operations of the 'Big Lift' type, Moscow has a considerable number of freight aircraft, which have proved their value carrying supplies for the re-equipment of Egypt's defeated army. It is clear from the Russian specialist press that a super-heavy aircraft with a carrying capacity of more than 100 tons, global range and high cruising speed is at present being developed.

In a political sense, the Kremlin has long been operating on an 'intercontinental' scale. Under the dual leadership of Leonid Brezhnev and Aleksey Kosygin, it has been doing so in accordance with definite geo-strategic concepts, which was not the case so long as Khrushchev was in power. The latter's policy was merely one of indiscriminate wooing of the 'third world'. We must expect Moscow to endeavour to gain a foothold in the vacuum created by Britain's withdrawal from 'east of Suez'. This is why Moscow is trying, not only in the Middle East but also in the Indian Ocean, South-East Asia and the Far East, to increase its political influence and, if possible, to establish new military positions there. A Soviet diplomatic offensive has begun in India, Burma, Cambodia, Malaysia, Singapore and Indonesia.

Wherever a chance offers, the Soviet Union makes use of military means to obtain bases as part of its 'global strategy'. In the meantime, the number of its 'clients' has grown very considerably. They are:

The Arab countries, which, as a return service, are opening up their ports to the Red Fleet operating in the Mediterranean and are probably also making airfields available to the Red Air Force units which are intended to provide support for the Soviet naval vessels in the Mediterranean.

India, which is being strengthened against the Chinese People's Republic.

North Vietnam and North Korea, which are at present active against Washington but may in future also become a nuisance to Peking.

Cyprus, which is a bone of contention between the NATO member States Greece and Turkey.

The Sudan and Nigeria, whom the Kremlin evidently regards as its best potential partners on the African continent.

This rough outline of past development may not be to everyone's liking; its truth, however, can hardly be contested. It would be difficult to find where precisely, in this general scheme of things, the non-proliferation treaty could fit in. The fact is that this treaty presupposes a degree of co-operation between the giants, whereas in actual fact their relations are, if anything, tending to become increasingly hostile. The simple question must be asked: Who is to protect the weak against the strong – who are growing stronger all the while? And yet it is the strong who are seeking protection from the weak – themselves to be kept weak! Since 'horizontal non-proliferation', which is the object of the exercise, seems all too obviously to go hand in hand with 'vertical proliferation', there is every justification for the weak to demand protection from the strong. But this demand has fallen on deaf ears, both in the Kremlin – which in any case regards the Geneva negotiations as nothing but a vehicle for its own ambitions directed against the Federal German Republic – and in the White House, which realizes that it is in no position to meet the have-nots' desire for greater security. There can be no doubt that the question of whether and how the signatories of the non-proliferation treaty will be rewarded in the shape of guarantees against 'nuclear blackmail' must be answered in the negative. 'Guarantees' depending on action by the Security Council can only be a farce, and the same is true of solemn declarations to the effect that neither will nuclear weapons be used, nor will their use be threatened, vis-à-vis the have-nots – as if the very existence of a nuclear potential did not in itself amount to potential blackmail!

The first point to establish is that the promises of protection which the nuclear Powers are being asked to make are to be given not in their own interests but, as it were, to please third parties. And since such promises would be bound to entail considerable risks, they would, from the outset, in view of their lack of credibility, be of scant value. The difficulties involved are quite obvious when one considers that what is meant by 'nuclear blackmail' cannot be precisely defined. In actual fact, any political demand made by a nuclear Power on a State which has no deterrent capability of its own is open to such an interpretation. If, for example, the USA were, for whatever reason, to exert serious pressure on a have-not country, the USSR would undoubtedly call this 'nuclear blackmail', since any intervention – e.g. in Vietnam or against a communist rising in Latin America – would, theoretically at least, entail the possibility of the use of means of mass destruction. On the other hand, if the Soviet Union were to threaten the use of force in whatever context, the USA would not consider this to be 'nuclear blackmail' so long as an ultimatum expressly threatening the use of nuclear weapons had not been issued. Experience shows, moreover, that world opinion tends to blame the Americans more for their military actions than it blames the Russians. As a result, Washington would be considerably restricted, by signing an international treaty of guarantee, in taking defence measures within its sphere of influence, while Moscow's room for manoeuvre would remain virtually intact.

This, then, is another reason why a universal agreement backed by a guarantee of the two Super-Powers would lead to a further 'erosion of NATO' within the European sphere. For the deterrent effect of the North Atlantic alliance depends to a considerable extent on the USA making it clear that it is its declared intention to use nuclear weapons even in the event of a purely conventional attack by the USSR should it prove impossible to halt such an aggression by any other means. There can be no doubt that this implies a threat on the part of Washington against Moscow – although, of course, a wholly passive threat. Soviet propaganda now says that this is an offensive strategy and that the USSR is being subjected to 'pressure'. It follows that if a guarantee agreement were really to come under serious discussion, the Kremlin would insist on an arrangement whereby the White House would have to give concrete assurances that nuclear weapons would only be used against nuclear weapons.

In Asia, a formal undertaking by the Great Powers aimed at giving cover to the small Powers against 'nuclear blackmail' would have even more problematical effects. The aim of such an undertaking would be, above all, to offer protection to India against the Chinese People's Republic. However, such a guarantee would be of value only in the event of New Delhi receiving guarantees against Chinese pressure from both Washington and Moscow. In practice, one can well imagine the Soviets letting the Americans act on their own to honour such a promise, thus involving the Americans in a direct conflict with the Chinese. The result of such a situation would be that the USSR would be in a position to take psychological, and possibly even military, advantage of America's use of nuclear weapons against its Chinese rivals. In the upshot, the USA would find itself serving Soviet interests. Any protective shield against 'nuclear blackmail' by Peking would be bound, by its very existence in international law as well as in view of the political uses that could be made of it, to be of advantage to Moscow and detrimental to Washington. It would have to be conceived as a means of 'containing' the yellow World Power and would thus primarily serve the interests of the Soviet Union since it would once and for all oppose the USA to China while the

USSR, unlike the USA, would always be able to evade any obligations that did not suit it.

Finally, a treaty of guarantee might also do harm inasmuch as crises which had heretofore been of local importance only would endanger the entire world as soon as one of the two Super-Powers became directly or indirectly involved. Such an agreement, which many have-nots desire for their own protection, could result in a confrontation of the two giants for trivial reasons. It is probable that in such an event the Americans would, in their own interest, have to come to an agreement with the Soviets and would thus have to take upon themselves a share of the responsibility for solutions which might not please those originally involved.

These arguments are essentially based on a US State Department analysis. They are the result of a dispassionate examination of the facts. The analysis arrives at the conclusion that there is an unbridgeable gulf between the motives of the Americans and those of the Russians. This, however, would seem to militate not only against an agreement offering direct guarantees to the have-nots against 'nuclear blackmail' but also against the non-proliferation treaty itself. The analysis proves that the Geneva negotiations lack the most important fundamental prerequisite: the ability and willingness of the two Great Powers to act in concert and to act for the good of the small States as a nuclear world police force.

In view of what has been happening, one is bound to ask oneself how long the 'relaxation of tension' between the super-powers, such as it is, can go on.

# 5     *Is there a 'Yellow Peril'?*

It would, I think, be wrong to assume that Soviet and American interests in Europe are gradually drawing closer in spite of the fact that the two Powers are inspired by different motives. The only point they have in common is their desire for a temporary 'standstill'. In other words – to use a geometrical simile – the lines of Moscow's and Washington's policies are not parallel, they cross. This is undoubtedly due both to the 'nuclear stalemate' and to the efforts of Peking, which, as I have mentioned, is also trying to assert itself as a World Power in order to upset the nicely laid schemes of Washington and Moscow.

These developments began to take shape during the second world war. As Japan was pushed back in China, the communist revolution gained speed, using, incidentally, American arms which Chiang Kai-Shek was forced to place at Mao Tse-tung's disposal in 1943–4 at the demand of the USA. The result was that not only was the foreign invader expelled but mainland China was conquered by the Communist Party and the USA driven out.

At first, the centre of world communism remained in Moscow, and this continued to be the case even after the Soviet leaders had begun to struggle among themselves for the succession following the death of Stalin. It was not long, however, before the USSR came to realize the risk – fully understood by Stalin – inherent in the export of communist revolution into new potential power centres with large populations. Peking began to demand a say within the communist bloc and to lay claim to leadership of the communist world. An ideological and imperial conflict (i.e. a clash of interests hinging both on the problem of how the doctrines of Marxism-Leninism should be applied in political affairs and on the Moscow-Peking rivalry for leadership) became inevitable. The Kremlin therefore found itself compelled to proclaim the formulae of 'relaxation' and 'coexistence' with the West, particularly after it had come to realize that the emergence of nuclear weapons had made the further expansion of world revolution by means of major wars impossible. But this happened only after a degree of equilibrium had been achieved in the nuclear sphere between the Soviet Union and the West. Henceforth the Soviets intended to confine their revolutionary activities to the support of wars of independence and liberation and to the fanning of revolutionary social unrest, especially in Africa, Asia and Latin America. As for Europe, the Soviets were for the time being content with the results achieved, their object being to use the status quo to extend their power westwards by new political methods.

China, which considered that its chances among the coloured peoples depended on its success in the contest with the white men of Moscow, was no longer prepared to subordinate its aims and methods to Soviet demands. When Khrushchev realized that a second leadership centre within the communist bloc was arising in Peking, he stopped Soviet technical and economic aid to China. He hoped thus to slow down, and if possible to stop altogether, the growth of China's power. His decision marked the emergence of polycentrism in the world communist camp. As a result, the power of the East was at first reduced.

As for the West, for the States associated in NATO, this development, if exploited carefully, appeared to offer a choice of genuine progress towards a relaxation in Europe. The NATO countries reacted accordingly. This gave rise to a commentary in the *Neue Zürcher Zeitung* of 16 August 1964 which I should like to quote in some detail:

The results are becoming visible of the new global constellation – the Washington-Moscow-Peking triangle – the results of which deserve our attention. At a time when this constellation was still only a subject for speculation, many European politicians and commentators expressed the hope that a future disintegration of the communist bloc, i.e. a Soviet-Chinese conflict, would bring benefits in the dispute between the West and the Soviets. It was assumed that, acting under the impact of its difficulties in the east, Moscow would have to shed some 'ballast' in the West and would thus become readier to listen to Western pleas for an acceptable settlement in Eastern and Central Europe.

Now that the conflict between Moscow and Peking has become a reality, there are many signs that events are in fact taking a different course. Instead of Moscow showing itself more ready to make concessions to the West, what is actually happening as a result of the Soviet-Chinese conflict is that Washington, and also London, are prepared to go to any length in order to make things easy for Moscow, in the belief that nothing must be done that might in the slightest degree promote a rapprochement between the two communist Powers. In fact, things have gone so far that some people – e.g. Sir Alec Douglas Home, speaking recently in the House of Commons – are beginning to talk of something like a community of interests between the West and the Soviet Union in the face of China's aggressive policies. It goes without saying all talk has ceased about the need to achieve, before anything else, an acceptable settlement of the problems which beset the Continent of Europe.

The fact that the point of gravity of American policy has shifted to Asia has resulted in the free world now being told that it is the Chinese brand of communism which is really dangerous and menacing while Soviet communism, the confrontation with which continues in Europe, is being presented as a problem which has to all intents already been mastered. For its part, Soviet propaganda is making great play with the yellow peril. Europe, however, has little reason to discount the Soviet peril on account of the yellow brand.

Modern academic opinion in fact supports the theory according to which the Chinese People's Republic alone threatens the world with aggressive and expansionist communism, while the Soviet Union is generally considered to be comparatively moderate and peaceable. Is this impression correct?

Is there really a 'yellow peril' which endangers all that is most sacred to the European peoples? Is Peking, which from time to time does behave like a frenzied, bloodthirsty dragon, really such an acute threat to world peace that not only China's immediate neighbours but also we who live a long way away should fear its actions? Is the boorish manner which Peking adopts in its diplomatic disputes proof that this Asian giant, who is still growing, is really totally bereft of reason and may therefore sooner or later blow the whole world sky-high? Are the mini-Maos at our universities, who grind out quotations from their great master on every conceivable occasion, really the harbingers of a world revolution which may bring down war on the whole of mankind?

There is no doubt that one could add to these questions *ad infinitum*. While Soviet actions are usually – and not always necessarily correctly – assumed by professional Kremlinologists to be rational, the Chinese attitude is thought to stem from irrational motives. A regime which instigates the young to create chaos in their country through a 'cultural revolution' appears to us to be in the throes of some diabolical frenzy. As for the 'Red Guards', whose activities seem to us to be an anarchical phenomenon, they have compounded this picture of China as an ogre capable of absolutely anything. The notion that this modern Genghis Khan might one day send his wild hordes across the border to destroy the present international order and make room for the establishment of a worldwide communist system fills us with fear. But realistic observers of the contemporary scene will have to agree that the disease of fanaticism, which Henry de Montherlant has so aptly called 'rabies of the mind', has its limits even in China. All plans of conquest, however passionately they may be cherished, require adequate resources for their execution. Mao Tse-tung's foreign policies have always shown that he realizes this. Consequently, he has never allowed his demoniac genius to tempt him into unrealistic ventures. Although his policies are expressed in strong language, they have in actual fact always been cautious: China only took part in the Korean war with 'volunteers'; she clearly pursued limited aims only in her Tibetan campaign in order to avoid a serious clash with Moscow; she called off her attack on India the moment it became clear that complete success was out of her reach; and she supports North Vietnam with propaganda rather than physical resources.

As regards Vietnam – judging by the situation as it appears in the spring of 1968 – it would seem that the United States has been drawn into a confrontation there with the Soviet Union rather than with Red China.

The assumption that the USSR could be persuaded to take on the job of mediator to ensure a fair outcome of the jungle war has all along been based on a strange error – the illusion that the Kremlin is just as honestly concerned to bring about a worldwide relaxation of tension as the White House. In actual fact, as I have noted before, the U S S R has always shown itself anxious to change the status quo in its own favour, while the U S A is bent on making it permanent. Consequently, Moscow still looks upon Washington as its arch-enemy, whom it seeks to harm whenever this can be done without endangering its own interests. Moscow therefore always takes the offensive wherever there is a chance and sends its 'clients' into the fray in order to cause its adversary, who invariably remains on the defensive, the maximum of losses through a process of attrition.

To realize this is to grasp that it is not an early conclusion of the Vietnam war, which the U S A is compelled to fight, but its continuation which would best serve the interests of the Soviet Union, both for politico-psychological and strategic-military reasons. There is no doubt that America's involvement on the side of South Vietnam is swallowing up American moral and material resources, while the Russians are in a position to estimate with some exactitude what advantages the East stands to gain from this situation at the expense of the West. The longer the conflict continues the more obvious it must become to Moscow that Washington is losing prestige both in its own camp and in the developing countries, the neo-isolationist moods are on the increase among the American public and that the North Atlantic Pact, which remains a thorn in Moscow's side as far as its ideas for Europe's future are concerned, is rapidly growing weaker. From the Soviet viewpoint, it therefore makes excellent sense to keep the Vietnamese pot on the boil and let the Americans stew in it until they are ready to eat. It is now known that between eighty and eighty-five per cent of the arms and other military equipment which Hanoi receives from abroad is supplied directly or indirectly by Moscow. The S A M rockets and the 800 A A guns supplied to North Vietnam by the Soviet Union have been inflicting considerable losses on the U S bombers in action there: on an average, 10 aircraft are lost over North Vietnam per 1,000 sorties, compared with 9.5 aircraft per 1,000 sorties in the second world war. Russia is able to test her modern armour and artillery in South Vietnam in battle conditions without having to risk the lives of her troops. When the Third Reich wanted to test its equipment in Spain, it had to send a volunteer legion into action; the Soviets, on the other hand, can use the blood of Viet Cong guerrillas and North Vietnamese troops.

Without Moscow's supplies and Soviet military advisers, Hanoi would hardly be able to sustain the fighting, with its ebb and flow of success and failure, for any length of time. If the Russians therefore really wanted to persuade their communist friends to change their tune and accept the offers of the Americans, they could no doubt do so without much trouble, the more so as this would presumably open up the way for the establishment of a Popular Front government in Saigon. The nightmare would soon be over in that event – at least for the time being – and Washington would be rid of an involvement which is a threat to its prestige.

But why should the Kremlin do Washington this favour? The Vietnam conflict is yielding rich dividends for Moscow at virtually no cost. The Soviet exchequer – using the state of affairs in the spring of 1968 as a base for our calculations – is, according to the lowest estimates, spending a mere £400 million annually on the U S S R's indirect participation in the Vietnam war, and £2,000 million according to the highest estimates, while only a handful of Soviet troops and technicians are active in Vietnam behind the front line as instructors. America, on the other hand, being directly involved, is having to make far greater sacrifices. The war cost her approximately £12,000 million in 1968 and was tying down 520,000 men in this theatre of operations – a total expected at the time to be raised still further. Moreover, a further 500,000 men were stationed at U S naval and air bases in the adjoining areas. In other words, what constitutes a heavy burden for the U S A, a burden which cannot and must not lightly be discarded, represents an attractive investment from the U S S R's point of view.

But would it not be even more attractive for Moscow to act as the peace-maker once again, as it did at Tashkent? This proposition, which people put forward from time to time, does not really bear examination. For at Tashkent, where the Soviet Union acted as mediator between India and Pakistan, it was not primarily concerned to build up her stock of international confidence – although, of course, it eventually pocketed the dividends in terms of enhanced prestige which came its way as a result of its mediation. Its main aim was to help settle a dispute that was liable to benefit China. But if the Kremlin were to intervene actively in favour of a settlement in Vietnam without obtaining anything in return, it would merely enable its yellow competitor to claim that the USSR had been aiding and abetting the White House. The Soviets would thus have to be naive indeed to do any such thing merely to make a good impression. It would take considerable concessions in terms of European territory – concessions which the Americans are in no position to offer – to induce Moscow to disregard the Chinese cries of 'traitor' and try to persuade the North Vietnamese by word and deed to enter into negotiations.

The position thus is that the Soviet Union is pocketing big dividends from the war – in view of the inability of the USA to offer it adequate concessions – considerably bigger dividends than those which are being enjoyed by the Chinese People's Republic. Assuming that Peking's noisy propaganda in favour of Hanoi is merely an obligatory ideological exercise, and if we consider solely the true political interests of the Middle Kingdom, we are bound to conclude that Mao Tse-tung is probably watching events with mixed feelings. It goes without saying that, on the one hand, he would like to see the 'white capitalists' driven from the areas around China. On the other hand, he can hardly wish to see a situation develop in which it would be easy for his comrades to the South, the Vietnamese, not only to reunite their own country but gradually to found an empire of their own by occupying Laos, Cambodia and Thailand. For this would help the Russians and harm the Chinese, a calculation based on the ancient wisdom that a giant is not worried by pygmies living on his doorstep but does not like anyone who is powerful to come too close, particularly if the latter should wish to ally himself with the giant's chief rival. To put it briefly: Red China may fear that in the long run she may find herself caught in a vice. The same applies, incidentally, to the relationship between the medium and small nation States of Europe and the USSR and vice versa.

The following further point should be borne in mind if one wishes to understand the game Moscow is playing in South-East Asia. The war which is now in progress there is not only helping Moscow's chances in its offensive against Washington; it also holds out the prospect to Moscow that it will be able to create a position, capable of further improvement, on which to base its defence against Peking.

Although the leader of the Red Middle Kingdom launched his 'proletarian cultural revolution' with incredible fanaticism, it must be assumed that he takes a coldly realistic view of the potential of his armed forces. He knows that the strength of his army lies in defence by means of guerrilla operations and that its weakness is its inability to conduct extensive conventional military operations in foreign territory. Although China's population exceeds 700 million, Mao's regular forces consist of a mere 2,300,000 troops. Of the 115 divisions of his army, only four are fully mechanized. Most of his artillery and armour is obsolete and, moreover, spares for this equipment are in short supply. As for his Air Force, which would have to act as the sword in any 'outward thrust', it is totally antiquated. In other words, he lacks the essential resources for an offensive. His manpower reserves – organized as militia – are estimated to total at least 50 million. They may provide a shield for defence but cannot at present be regarded as a suitable instrument for expansion.

On the other hand, the Chinese People's Republic is maturing into a nuclear Power more swiftly than was at first assumed. In June 1967, Peking slapped down on the table of the UN, which was at that time trying to achieve a peace settlement in the Middle East, its thermo-nuclear trump card in order to make it clear to all and sundry that China was ready to take part in the big game whether people liked it or not. There can be no doubt that in exploding its first hydrogen bomb when it did, the Chinese People's Republic was out to create a political and propaganda effect in Asia. It wanted to show that the United States and the Soviet Union were no longer on their own in deciding the destinies of any part of the world but must henceforth allow others, too, to have a say. The choice of the exact time for the experiment was undoubtedly connected with the crisis in the Eastern Mediterranean then in progress – i.e. Mao Tse-tung was clearly eager to impress the Arabs, who felt that they had been let down by the Kremlin. But in mounting her sixth nuclear test, China was certainly motivated by more than a simple desire to produce a momentary psychological effect. Her aim clearly was to show the world that she was strong enough to step up the rate of her nuclear development. Evidently, the Red Middle Kingdom not only has adequate supplies of fissionable materials but also the necessary production capacity to take in hand the serial output of nuclear weapons. The production potential which the Chinese are constructing has now passed the rudimentary stage.

The experts realized that it would be foolish to delude oneself about the shape of things to come as long ago as 26 October 1966, for on that day Peking succeeded in firing a guided missile with a payload of at least 100,000 tons of TNT equivalent into a target 400 miles away. And since the experiment was a success, it must be assumed that both the missile and the explosive used are now in serial production. Experts predict that before long the Chinese will have a stock of 150 to 200 short-range missiles, each capable of carrying a minimum payload of 20,000 tons of TNT equivalent. By the end of the decade – since it now has thermo-nuclear warheads available – Peking is likely to start producing medium-range missiles (range 2,200 miles). This would mark the transition from tactical to strategic nuclear weapons, and it must be assumed that by 1975 China will have built her first ICBMs, missiles with a range of 6,000 miles, as well as hydrogen bomb warheads with an explosive power in the megaton range. This 'time schedule' rests on the assumption that Peking will continue to spend several hundred million pounds annually on nuclear research, as well as appropriate sums on research for the development of missiles and electronic devices.

One of the early justifications for the controversial ABM system was against Chinese rockets. But why should the Chinese defence attack the Americans, since they would stand to gain nothing by so doing but might lose a great deal? It will be a long time before Peking can contemplate a large-scale war with Washington, since, in the event of such a war, it would be at the mercy of Moscow. There can be no doubt that the USSR would not make its aid available free of charge if such a war were to occur, so that Mao's empire would soon be in trouble and faced with the alternative of either allowing itself to be smashed or of once again submitting – as the price of Soviet assistance – to the will of the Kremlin. The Russians would all the better be able to enforce such a demand as it is certain that they would also be offered all sorts of concessions by the Americans once a US-Chinese clash appeared imminent. It cannot be Mao's intention, or that of his successors, to place China's chief rival in so favourable a position.

Peking's aim in making such extraordinary efforts to acquire means of mass destruction is more likely to be a desire to intimidate the Russians. The contingency the Chinese have in mind is that one day China might feel herself strong enough – protected by a future nuclear stalemate – to attempt a northward expansion. There can be no doubt that this is what China, whose population is likely to reach the 1,000 million mark by the year 2,000, is driving at.

Even more than by ideological conflict, China and Russia are separated by '5,500 miles of enmity', for that is the length of the disputed boundary between the two communist giants, reckoning the Mongolian People's Republic as politically part of the U S S R. That frontier stretches from the bitterly cold regions of Northern Manchuria, with their pine forests and rivers, to the dusty deserts of Turkestan. Along this line of demarcation, which the Russians show clearly on their maps but which is only shaded in as undetermined on Chinese maps, Moscow is at present reported to have stationed about forty divisions, facing some fifty to sixty Chinese divisions.

Four hundred years ago China and Russia were still separated by an area more than 2,000 miles wide. But the hordes of Mongol and Turkic peoples – mostly nomads – living in Central Asia, were eventually conquered either by Moscow or Peking. Finally, during the nineteenth century, the two countries closed the gap and became contiguous. Subsequently, Moscow began to cut into the territories controlled by Peking. The Tsars made inroads into the territories of the Manchu Dynasty, reducing the area of the Middle Kingdom by a total of 695,000 square miles, of which much more than half is to this day in Soviet hands. In other words, Russian imperialism, which had such devastating effects in Europe after the second world war, also inflicted considerable territorial losses on China.

Mao Tse-tung has from the outset declared the treaties concluded by the Tsars and the Manchu Emperors to have been 'unequal'. However, during the time when he appeared to be on friendly terms with Josef Stalin, Mao seemed disposed to accept the Amur as the frontier between the two countries. Later, however – after the dispute between Peking and Moscow had broken out – he made more far-reaching demands. He hinted that it was

73

his intention, 'when the time is ripe', to revive his claim to Vladivostok, to the Soviet Far Eastern provinces and to certain areas of Soviet Central Asia said to be 'oppressed' by the USSR. Mao has repeatedly spoken of Russian excesses in Eastern Siberia, commenting grimly: 'We have not yet presented our accounts for settlement.'

Marshal Chen Yi used an even more threatening tone. He called the Russians 'thieves' who had filched 580,000 square miles of land from his people. Chen Yi said this in May 1966. Mao himself – the leader of an over-populated country – pointed out shortly afterwards that it was 'immoral' from a geo-political point of view that vast areas of land should be inhabited by sparse populations. There can be little doubt that the Russians have by now begun to feel uncomfortable about all this, for Moscow's Far Eastern provinces, covering an area of 1,160,000 square miles, have a population of only some 6,000,000. These territories present a great temptation to Peking, particularly in view of their considerable mineral wealth.

Politically, the Russian-Chinese dispute is, if anything, of advantage to Europe, for to us Europeans the 'Red peril' must still appear more dangerous than the yellow brand, especially since it is the Soviet Union and not China which occupies European territories.

Is it not necessary, therefore, to turn the Moscow-Peking-Washington triangle, mentioned by *Neue Zürcher Zeitung*, into a quadrangle by including Europe in the configuration in order to even out the balance of forces in our favour? If we are to do this, the political unity of our continent must first be achieved. How important this could be for a solution of our problems was indicated by Mao Tse-tung himself when he referred, in denouncing Russia's aggressive and annexationist ambitions, to the occupation of parts of Eastern Europe by the Soviet Union.

For all this, Peking will certainly not become our ally. However, if we examine the situation pragmatically, we are bound to come to the conclusion that Red China has an interest in seeing a focus of power established along the western borders of the Soviet empire in Central Europe; for our part, we are interested in seeing more of the Soviet potential tied down along the USSR's East

Asian frontier. Hence, our interests and those of China do meet, albeit only partially and temporarily.

In this connection, it is amusing to note that the question keeps cropping up, among the leaders of the CPSU and in Soviet diplomatic circles, whether Bonn and Peking may not one day begin to co-operate. It is hinted that such a development would be very annoying and that the prospect is anything but pleasant. On the other hand, the feeling seems to be that the Federal Republic is too dependent on the USA to be able to afford such a machiavellian policy – a scarcely veiled hint at the existence of a special community of interests between Washington and Moscow. Two particularly interesting articles have appeared in this connection in the Moscow weekly *Literaturnaya Gazeta*, in the issues of 10 and 17 April 1968 respectively. The articles are by the Soviet journalist Rostovsky, who is not only a political commentator but also a semi-official spokesman. He originally became known through two books which he published in the West in the thirties under the pseudonym 'Ernest Henri'. In their English-language versions the books appeared under the titles *Hitler Over Europe* and *Hitler Over Russia*. He speaks of the fear which haunts the Russians that one day their European and Asian enemies may decide to make common cause. He describes the Federal Republic and Red China as the two outsiders of world politics and goes on to say that there are good reasons for believing that Peking and Bonn are beginning to attract one another and that this is no mere coincidence. However much this warning may owe to Russian fear of an unholy alliance, and however little justification there may be for it in actual fact, it is nevertheless noteworthy that these remarks have been published by a political commentator in present-day Russia – a country which throughout centuries of its history has always pretended to be haunted by the fear of external attack and which, supposedly in order to buttress its 'security', kept on conquering more and more territory which it then proceeded to swallow up 'for security reasons'. Thus Russia now stands in the heart of Germany and Europe, still clamouring for 'security' in the face of the 'militarist, revanchist and aggressive Federal Republic'.

It goes without saying that no reasonable person would suggest that we should blindly entrust our fate to the Chinese dragon in the hope that it will one day free us from the embrace of the Russian bear. It is equally obvious – and no one seriously doubts – that despite the fact that our interests sometimes clash, the United States is our most valued ally and will remain so, an ally whose interests must be given due weight. What I wish to say is that, in the first place, the resistance of the Chinese to the Soviets helps to strengthen our political defence, for the Chinese attitude provides us with hard and fast factual – and not just elaborately constructed – arguments against the supposedly realistic demand that we should recognize the European status quo. Secondly, I believe that we shall have a chance of taking the political offensive – to some extent thanks precisely to the Soviet-Chinese conflict – as soon as Europe has become united on the basis of the long-term identity of her interests. This will make her sufficiently strong to function as a politically active element in the world. No longer will she be the passive object of the actions of others or, worse still, be accused of disturbing the peace.

# 6 *Relaxation of Tension in Europe*

Moscow and Washington's 'identity' of interests – although as I have pointed out, these interests do not in fact run parallel but are at odds with one another – has made Europe into a passive object in the hands of the giants because those who are responsible for its fate have so far lacked the courage to take the plunge, to jump over the shadow of their countries' past as nation States and to amalgamate Europe's splintered forces. If this were done the economic power of such a European federal State would be greater than the sum total of the several potentials of the existing nation States. Are things to remain as they are, will the two super-powers continue to improvise solutions of the problems which face them, solutions which take little account of Europe's needs? For us Europeans it is not a case of taking over the burdens which the USA has to bear in other parts of the world and to try to play at 'world politics'. What we must do is to make sure that we do not step by step lose the right to decide our own fate. At the moment, we are still permitted, to some extent, to share in the processes of decision-making. However, this can only mean that the concept of national sovereignty as it used to be understood has gone with the wind so far as Europe is concerned and can only be recovered in a new form if Europe takes the road of supranational amalgamation. Once we have lost all influence over events in the European area, others will make the decisions about Europe's anachronistic world of miniature States and Europeans will be left with nothing but their traditional formal sovereignty.

For Europe's old world is situated between the two fronts – right at the centre of the area of tension between the two contending forces – now supposedly in a state of 'relaxation'. It is up to us

Europeans to realize what the consequences must inevitably be if the two super-powers mutually guarantee the status quo in Europe – the eastern partner in order to be able to alter it in its own favour at a later date, and the western in the belief that in this way the balance of power can be stabilized and peace preserved.

The division of Europe, and the partition of Germany into two States, will come to be seen as a prerequisite for the continued existence of the equilibrium the two nuclear giants have adopted as the basic theme of their respective policies, although for very different reasons. The Soviet Union has defined its 'minimum' conditions for a guaranteed delimitation of the Soviet and US spheres of influence in Europe very clearly. Washington, on the other hand, which is loath publicly to disavow the ideal of European unity and, moreover, is alive to the obligations, both moral and legal, which it has taken on vis-à-vis the German people, now finds itself in a difficult position. If America is to be saved from further exposure to strong Moscow pressure and enabled to remain loyal to the principles of its European policy, Europeans can do nothing better than make it clear to the whole world, and especially to the United States, that they are determined to pursue an independent policy. It is thus up to us Europeans to act. In so doing, we must take as our point of departure the following conviction, which we cannot stress too much in our discussions with our Atlantic allies: 'What is good for the cause of Europe's political consolidation and independence cannot but benefit the United States of America.'

In the last few years profound changes have taken place in world politics, changes which should make us realize that time is now running short for Europe. When the Treaty of Rome was signed, it was not yet clear how soon the changes in the strategic situation of the United States would produce drastic, even fateful, consequences for our continent. It was only when America's military involvement on her Pacific flank began to grow in scale that it became unmistakably clear that Europe must speed up its action, and must do so effectively, if she were to unite and assert her identity. She must no longer remain content to await the birth of a political community of the European peoples through the evolutionary process of economic coalescence. It is not only the new situation in the Atlantic system but also the changes which have been set in motion in our continent which now place before the peoples of Western Europe as a priority task the need to establish an identity of national interests with their respective neighbours and to make the whole of their newly recovered strength fully available for Europe's consolidation and unity. This applies to the members of the EEC, who first formulated the concept of a political union, as well as to all the other States of Europe which are free to act and decide independently. The sooner the free countries of our continent – and especially the Six – join forces in a common foreign and defence policy, thus incidentally providing a protective umbrella for the internal growth of the EEC, the more clearly we shall see the contours emerge of a future great Europe.

It is therefore nothing less than tragic that Europe's progress towards political unity has been marking time for some years now. The reasons are: our inability to agree on Britain's accession to the EEC; France's belief that the development of the Common Market and unrestricted national sovereignty can be combined and that, moreover, she is entitled to act on behalf of Europe in world affairs without having received a mandate so to do; Holland and Belgium's rejection of de Gaulle's claim to the leadership of Europe and their flirtation with Britain. Moreover, the Federal Republic – as the strategically most important, economically strongest but politically weakest country of Europe, fighting as it is to overcome its past – is trying to be all things to all men, and at the same time, to be as inconspicuous as possible.

America is so busy with the problems of her own stability and external security that she is no longer able to involve herself fully in support of her friends' interests. The Americans realize very well that they are near the limit of their forces, beyond which they cannot discharge the obligations which they have undertaken or which have been imposed on them. This is particularly clear in two areas – in connection with the guarantee that the USA will use its deterrent on behalf of overseas peoples, and in regard to the stability of the dollar. It is up to the nations of Western Europe, allied to the United States in a spirit of freedom, to take effective action in these areas. This, of course, they can neither do singly nor at the expense of their common security.

A bipolar East-West 'relaxation' must result in a weakening of the free world. Any legal or diplomatic recognition of the status quo, such as Moscow is systematically working for, is intended not only to legalize the demarcation line agreed at Yalta and thus put the seal of the partition of Germany into two States but also to prevent Europe from becoming an independent Power. It is our duty as Germans and Europeans to extricate our American partners from this dilemma. A 'policy of relaxation' based on the idea of a 'European collective security system' as promoted by Moscow would not be worthy of the name. What the East is really doing is trying to undermine the Western positions. The Kremlin is attempting to create a belt of neutral States stretching from Scandinavia to Italy, with the Federal Republic as its nucleus. I am firmly convinced that all the tactical moves which the East has been making in connection with Germany have been undertaken with this in mind.

In view of this precarious position – into which we are to be driven by the Soviets' active policy of coexistence – it is up to us to adopt an active policy of our own. If we were to rely on our own devices and remain chained to America as our protective Power, we should be helpless. One day we might be at the mercy of the influence and decisions of a superior Eurasian Power. It is therefore up to us to create the basis for our own policy of European relaxation in opposition to that of the East. We must establish the nucleus of a political community of action in Western Europe, capable of developing into an independent Power, a Power which would both be recognized as an ally by Washington and accepted as a negotiating partner by Moscow. Already there is surreptitious talk in Western capitals that we Germans are trying to prove, by pursuing a foreign policy of our own based entirely on the alliance with Washington, that our ties with the West are inadequate to protect German interests. We are suspected of trying in this way to create an alibi for a new 'Rapallo'. We must beware, above all else, of a crisis of confidence within our own camp, for such a crisis would have an immediate and massive impact on the Federal Republic.

What we Germans need is roots in a strong and independent Europe. This Europe must be an element of equilibrium in world affairs. In other words, one of our tasks must be to make this design for Europe palatable to the communist world.

It is, in any case, our duty to pursue a flexible foreign policy wherever possible. But to believe that Moscow will allow itself to be swept off its feet by the events of the last few years and will permit its European satellites to set up a liberal system which would give them the freedom to make their own political decisions, would be a dangerous delusion. The Soviet Union will never relinquish control and leadership of its sphere of influence without being compelled to do so by political developments in the rest of the world.

Anyone who thought that the Soviet attitude had undergone a fundamental change since the brutal crushing of the Hungarian freedom movement in 1956 must have been bitterly disappointed by the Soviet military intervention on 21 August 1968 in response to the process of democratization in Czechoslovakia. I take the following view of this development, which occurred shortly before this book went to press:

1. It would be a dangerous mistake to believe that the process of democratization which has taken place in a number of East European countries is the result of the West's policy of relaxation. This process is in fact an inevitable response to the system in force in Eastern Europe; in other words, it is inherent in that system. By this I do not mean to say that the Western policy of relaxation which has been pursued up to now vis-à-vis the involuntary members of the Warsaw Pact is wrong. All I wish to do is to issue a warning against the misconceived notion that there is a causal link there.

2. The West's exaggerated enthusiasm for relaxation at any price made it easier for the Soviet Union to decide on an intervention in Czechoslovakia on 21 August 1968 because it gave rise to the dangerous idea in the Soviet Union that it had become the 'greatest' of all Powers and could afford to look upon the USA as being far from superior, not even equal to, the USSR.

3. It would also be mistaken to think that the Soviets were unaware of the risk of worldwide condemnation of their action. What they did know for certain was that they were running no military risk – that the danger of such an intervention was even smaller than it was in 1956 in Hungary – and, having taken a hard, realistic look at the pros and cons of their proposed action, decided

81

to go ahead with it on 21 August. In fact, they had been preparing for this step with meticulous care since the end of June 1968. This is obvious from some of their advance measures: mobilization of reservists in the Soviet Union's Western Military Region; creation of a huge military machine for use both as a means of pressurizing Czechoslovakia and as an army of intervention; the launching of the manoeuvres code-named 'Operation Bohemian Forest' – a cover for the military encirclement of Czechoslovakia which preceded the lightning invasion; the establishment of closed areas – e.g. in Saxony at the end of June 1968; the construction of emergency airfields and military supply dumps; the construction of fortifications in accordance with an emergency programme which, according to witnesses, was carried out with a speed and on a scale that can only be compared with the construction of Hitler's Western Wall. We should do well in connection with all this to beware of imagining that the Kremlin leaders are in any way actuated by the same thoughts and sentiments which move the Western world.

4. The Soviets clearly heeded Bismarck's dictum about Bohemia being the 'key to Europe'. They were prepared to risk whatever might be in store for them – the hatred of the Czech people; the reaction in Rumania and Yugoslavia; the condemnation of their action by the majority of communist parties outside the Warsaw Pact; the disappointment of the politicians favouring 'relaxation'; the danger that the non-proliferation treaty might never be signed; setbacks in the non-aligned world, etc. Why were they prepared to accept all these risks? Because, with China knocking at their back door, they felt that action was called for on their other flank in Europe! They have now positioned their military forces to give support to a policy in the success of which they have more faith than many a European politician, i.e. a policy aimed at producing a final settlement in Europe in their own favour. However that may be, the menacing shadow they have thrown across Europe will enable them increasingly to influence future decisions about the fate of a Europe which has been weakened by unilateral measures of disarmament and which no longer enjoys unconditional U S backing, including U S willingness to accept the risk of nuclear war. Against this background it becomes understandable why the Soviets have made no official comment on the so-called 'European

option', which has been mooted in connection with the non-proliferation treaty, and have actually rejected it semi-officially. What we do know for certain is that Europe, even should it succeed in establishing its political unity, is to be deprived of the right to make any decisions regarding its own armament.

The relations between Moscow and the East European States have unquestionably undergone certain changes. In the economic sphere, and particularly in foreign trade, there are many signs that these countries need no longer necessarily be viewed as 'satellites'. However, the room for political manoeuvre which Moscow allows its 'allies' remains limited, and the unity of the 'socialist camp' is still a reality which the Soviets are determined to maintain in being even at the cost of military intervention, as their recent action in Czechoslovakia has shown. The relative 'freedom' which Moscow is prepared to allow these countries in their contacts with the West must to some extent be considered a consequence of current technical, economic and social developments. At the same time, the point of gravity of Moscow's political tactics has shifted, the U S S R's aim being to increase its influence in other parts of Europe. It is up to us to counter these tactics.

No doubt, the communist world is at present going through a phase of internal evolution. The processes taking place in the Eastern bloc, variously described as 'liberalization' and 'democratization', are in themselves no reason for excessive Western optimism; this much we can see from the example of Czechoslovakia. This phase may come to an end long before anything approaching democracy or genuine freedom has emerged victorious behind the Iron Curtain. Economic deficiencies and setbacks, as well as growing national awareness, have called forth among the present generation a massive demand for a higher standard of living. Automation and the growth of industrial production have had certain sociological effects; a middle class of technical functionaries and officials, of technicians and automation experts, has emerged. This has in turn given rise to a dynamic process which the West should support. Though it would be wrong to speak of a bourgeoisie, there can be no overlooking the fact that a new, independent élite has come into being in Eastern Europe.

Stronger cultural and trade relations with these States could

D

promote these tendencies. True, our export trade with them is largely financed out of loans, but this is a difficulty which the West will have to overcome. We will have to find ways and means of turning the situation to our own political advantage. This means that the West should only back projects which tend to foster the links between the divided parts of Europe rather than schemes designed to promote the economic strength of the East European regimes. The EEC Powers, which are in any case under an obligation to work out a joint trade policy by 1970 at the latest, should give priority to the important task of formulating a common policy for trade with the East. In this connection, a start should be made by agreeing a joint credit policy; our Eastern neighbours would then have to recognize the EEC as a trading partner. This would have a psychological effect, especially on those East European countries which are eager to establish closer ties with the West. Moreover, if this is done, it will become impossible for the East to play off one Western country against another. A particularly effective move would be to set up the EEC's Office for Trade with the East in West Berlin. This would in no way prejudice the four-Power status of, and the guarantee of the three Western Powers for, Berlin – on the contrary! As for the East European countries, they would in this way learn to accept the European community as a fact. However, all this presupposes that Western Europe will produce a co-ordinated policy. The idea of one Europe will only become feasible if it is based on solid foundations in Western Europe.

A political rapprochement with the East, be it in the economic or the diplomatic sphere, can only produce positive results if it is based on such foundations. Admittedly, bilateral agreements have their uses, especially when they are based on traditional relationships between European countries in the Western and Eastern camps; however, such agreements must be backed by an agreed West European policy. Otherwise the East might exploit these individual contacts in order to undermine Western unity. There can be no question that this is one of the reasons for the Soviet Union allowing the countries of Eastern Europe a semblance of political latitude.

Our task thus is to draw our Eastern neighbours closer to Europe. But it would be wrong to delude oneself that by means of medium

84

and long-range credits – without which trade relations cannot be strengthened – by giving technical advice, industrial aid and economic assistance, these countries can gradually be turned from dictatorships into democracies. We must, therefore, be alert to the danger that this economic co-operation may enable the communist governments to consolidate their regimes and reconcile their populations to the harshness of life under a dictatorship. It must be our endeavour to encourage in these countries the evolution which I have described, the first beginnings of which can now be discerned, and to foster it until it has reached the point where a return to the old Stalin-type methods of terror will become unthinkable.

I believe it to be wrong to keep on talking about Germany's reunification while overlooking the crux of the problem and glossing over the real issues. Our problem is not merely the partition of Germany but also the division of Europe. We should bear in mind that Poland, Czechoslovakia, Hungary, Bulgaria, Rumania, etc., are just as much part of Europe as Switzerland, Holland or Belgium. It is up to us to see to it, both by exerting an influence on these countries and by patient negotiation with Moscow, that these countries become part of Europe again – to begin with in the sense reflected in the expression 'intermediate Europe'.

How effective such a European policy of relaxation could be can be seen from the Soviet reaction to General de Gaulle's policies. Moscow watched the increased contacts between France and several member States of the Warsaw Pact with evident displeasure. Foreign Minister Gromyko made a point of visiting Paris in order to make it clear to the French, to the USSR's East European satellites and to the world at large that if such negotiations were to be held at all, Moscow was the capital to approach, and not Warsaw, Prague or Budapest.

Yet, there can be no question that a relaxation in Europe as a whole cannot be achieved against Moscow's will. But the greater the force of attraction exercised by an independent Western Europe upon the States of Central and Eastern Europe, the sooner will Moscow be ready to tread the same path. The longer Western Europe delays establishing its unity, the longer will Moscow pursue another policy: it will try to persuade the French that any collaboration with Germany is dangerous and that Paris would be better advised to get rid of its German partner and to revert to its historic alliance with Moscow, Warsaw and Prague, and also, of course to press for an American withdrawal from Europe – a Europe which would then be ripe for neutralization.

If this were to happen the isolation of the Federal Republic would be as good as an accomplished fact and a further hurdle would have been placed in the path of the reunification and unity of Europe. The maintenance of the status quo would in that case be assured. Moscow also knows perfectly well, however, that the implications of a united Europe have to be assessed in twentieth century terms and that, were a third Great Power to emerge, it would have to be treated on a par with the USA.

The aim of the policy which we Europeans should follow must in the last analysis, be to induce Moscow to choose between Red China, Europe and America. Either the Kremlin will then decide in favour of Peking, which, at best, would mean that Moscow would have to share the leadership of the communist world with the Asian giant; at worst, it would have to reconcile itself to playing second fiddle for a long time to come and would have to give in to China's demands. Alternatively, the Kremlin may succeed in establishing a fundamental understanding with the other two World Powers, America and Europe. The decisive point to bear in mind in this connection is that there can be no satisfactory solution if Europe is excluded from such a political constellation. While the Soviets and the Americans remain seated at the conference table on their own, the present world balance of power will remain unchanged, and this would still be the case even if these two Powers were to meet regularly.

One thing, it is to be hoped, is clear to all those who occupy positions of political responsibility in Western Europe, i.e. that Moscow will use all the means at its disposal – flattery and threats, promises and pressure, propaganda and blackmail – to prevent the creation of a European Great Power. In examining the situation in the world today, the Kremlin strategists can see that Russia has three flanks – the USA, China and Europe. The USA is the great adversary, the world's greatest economic and military Power. It is ready to conclude an arrangement with the USSR on the basis of a de facto recognition of the status quo; nevertheless, its presence is irksome and could in certain circumstances become dangerous. China is the hostile brother who is clamouring with increasing insistence for the right to lead the communist world, while at the same time making territorial claims and marching forward to the status of a world nuclear Power. As for a united Europe, it would undoubtedly be a democratic, and not a communist, Power. On the other hand, it must be assumed that Moscow does not relish the thought of even a communist united Europe, since, by virtue of its population and economic potential, it would create an additional danger from the West, imperilling Moscow's leadership of the communist world. The emergence of a democratic Europe would be even less to Moscow's liking, for it does not want to see a United States of Europe – especially one allied to the United States of America – emerge as the Eastern bloc's western neighbour. Moscow is well aware that it would be impossible to neutralize such a Europe and to turn it into a power vacuum, and it also knows that such a Europe would have a tremendous attraction for its eastern neighbours. Moreover, it would then become impossible to go on invoking the so-called 'German threat' and to use it as a means of holding the bloc together. Such a Europe would cause a shift in the world balance of power – the only shift which could conceivably benefit the democratic world. But how far should this Europe – which must be fashioned into a single unit – extend if we are to preserve its special character, reflected in the diversity of its members? Should it not also include Russia?

In terms of geography and cultural history, it may be quite true that Europe does stretch from the Atlantic to the Urals, but anyone who is prepared to look at the historical changes that have occurred during the course of this century must agree that it is inconceivable that Europe as a political concept and political proposition should extend beyond the present western frontier of the Soviet Union. Moreover, as a Power extending into Asia, the USSR would carry so much weight that, even leaving aside the question of its social order – so firmly established there – and the matter of its ideological objectives, a common Europe which included the USSR could never be established.

I simply cannot take de Gaulle's reference to a 'Europe from the Atlantic to the Urals' literally, but interpret it as a plea that the countries of Eastern Europe ought not to be excluded from the continent's unification. Therefore, in regard to unification, it is our aim to ensure that those countries which belong to Europe and which are able, ready and willing shall one day be helped to move closer to a West European State. To create that State, to promote its emergence through a common policy, the adoption of which must precede the creation of such a State, is a task and a duty facing the countries of Western Europe, which are in a position to choose their political path in relative freedom. It is no use trying to run before one can walk.

The peoples of Eastern and South-Eastern Europe, who today are still under Soviet political and military control, are certain to have understood the meaning of de Gaulle's initiative. The longing for freedom and national self-determination which is fermenting in these countries, reflects not only their desire to recover their lost right to shape their own lives but also their wish to become members of an all-European community of peoples. This longing for independence and this hope for the realization of a great, viable united Europe can, however, only be fulfilled if a process of political consolidation is carried forward in the West. The people of Eastern Europe are looking to us and expect the free part of the continent – which alone is in a position at present to act and decide freely in favour of an independent European policy – to create the foundations of a future great European community.

To sum up. We cannot leave the cause of East-West relaxation in the European area to those World Powers which are responsible for having drawn up the line of demarcation at Yalta. We seek and desire relaxation, security and peace. We realize, however, that we cannot achieve these objectives on the basis of a status quo founded on the division of our continent and the partition of Germany. Consequently, European policy must not be allowed to remain a function of America's policy of security, which is based on a complex of interests different from ours. At the same time, European policy must be so devised as to help push back and weaken Soviet influence over the destinies of our peoples. Only when a policy that is complete within itself has been formulated, a policy which will allow us to act systematically, each playing his own part, shall we Europeans be able to work for a relaxation with the East. Western Europe must continue to press for the independence and autonomy which would attract and fire the imagination of the peoples of Eastern Europe so that the latter's longing for self-determination will reinforce our endeavour to create a great all-European political union.

# 7    *A Europe of the Nations?*

The German question is at the heart of the problem of Europe's unity, and it therefore seems right to examine and treat it, not simply as a German national aspiration requiring international backing (such support may in any case be largely confined to lip service to the principle of self-determination for all the world's peoples), but rather as a matter of concern to Europe as a whole. The first question we must ask ourselves is: What exactly can a 'nation' achieve nowadays as a political institution?

It is not the Germans alone who must inject new meaning into the concept of nationhood and give it a new image in the present era of profound structural changes throughout the world. The great nations of Europe which achieved their own statehood were able to exert a crucial influence on the course of modern history. But only those 'classical' nation States which were large enough to absorb the effects of the process of industrialization that took place in the nineteenth and the first half of the twentieth century were able to do this. These States had to be large enough to allow a sense of community to evolve dynamically on the basis of a common language, cultural traditions and historical background. Reflecting, in a sense, the ruthlessness and group egoism typical of the new, big industrial enterprises, there emerged national imperialism, which was destined to mark the beginning of the end of this era with the first, and to bury it with the second, world war.

Once the historian has succeeded, in his examination of the past, in correctly relating technological and social to political developments, he will perceive the real – functional – character of the nation State. The abundant romantic trimmings with which it used to be the custom to embellish this type of society will then be seen as having been designed to fill a psychological need, the idea being to promote the cohesion and power of the nation concerned. Viewed from this angle, a nation State is a community based on common interest which seeks to assert itself against the outside world, keeps at bay harmful foreign influences and harnesses and organizes its own resources as best possible. The more successful a nation State was in these efforts, the more strongly did its citizens develop their 'national pride' – a distinct sense of belonging to a group whose members resemble one another and who know how to assert themselves in the world, how to mould their own destiny and gain the respect of foreigners.

In this way, the idea gained ground that a nation can only enjoy the right of self-determination in full measure if it possesses the attributes of full sovereignty, which must be reflected in the existence of a State led – and if possible named after – the nation in question. Governments have always been eager to make their subjects believe that the independence and welfare of their nation State is not only essential to the exercise of their right of self-determination and to their prosperity, but that the existence of such a State is virtually synonymous with such a situation. History has shown this proposition to be both wrong and insincere. There are nations which have achieved democracy, with all its obligations, as well as economic prosperity, within the framework of a nation State; there are others which have attained these ends within a multi-national State; others still have had to suffer oppression and misery under either of these systems.

The creation, preservation and promotion of the influence of the nation State – which many have come to regard, without valid reason, as being synonymous with 'the fatherland' – has inspired men to intense emotions and great deeds. The effort to create a sense of identity between the concepts of State and nation and to mobilize in this way the irrational urges of a people whose members consider themselves bound together by a common destiny in view of their common traditions, customs and ability to communicate with one another, and to harness these forces within the framework of a rational order of society, may well have a claim to being regarded as an inspiring and reasonable undertaking. However, there has always been another side to this coin: the potential danger that the nation State may give rise to unrestrained group egoism stemming from an uncritical attitude towards one's own nation. This, in turn, may lead to the nation's isolation, brought about either deliberately or unintentionally.

The evil excesses of nationalism, which the German people have experienced in a particularly outrageous form and for which even a generation which had no part in them is to this day being held responsible by the outside world, grew from the concept of the hegemony of the nation State. Nationalism was destined to become the gravedigger of a Europe organized as a patchwork of States, but this is not to say that it is the nation States which have been exclusively, or even predominantly, guilty of internal or external terror. There are sufficient examples available – some taken from recent history – which clearly show how false and one-sided such a view would be. On the other hand, however, there can be no doubt that a people is most liable to become burdened with guilt and opprobrium when it is organized as a nation State.

The Germans, who achieved their own national statehood belatedly and in an incomplete form as recently as the final third of the last century, were to experience the negative effects of this type of system in an extreme form. Under the guidance of irresponsible leaders, they were asked to give their all, supposedly for the common good. In the end it turned out that the sacrifices, which the majority had made from a genuine sense of solidarity, had not only been pointless but had been exploited for one of the worst crimes in mankind's history. As a result of the bitter realization of what had happened, the national feelings of the German people suffered severe – but let us hope not lasting – damage.

The trauma of the National Socialist fiasco led the Germans from a peak of boundless self-esteem, induced by a so-called nationalist 'philosophy', into an abyss of universal contempt. Thereafter, everything that smacked in the slightest of the national ideal was proclaimed anathema in German literature and in the press. German unity was destroyed by a brutal act of partition. As a result of all this, the Germans were almost brought to the point of being ashamed of their own national identity. The willingness of the German people to shoulder the necessary share of responsibility for the preservation of the nation's cultural values and gifts has thus been dangerously weakened.

All this goes to show how dangerous it is for a nation to think that it can fulfil itself only within its own State. To believe this is to accept that any failure of its nation State is proof that a nation is incapable of continued existence. The Germans would be wrong to allow their disappointment over the setback they suffered during the final phase of Europe's nation-State era – a failure which was due to the historical and geographical circumstances of the time, coupled with faults of their own – to cloud their judgement. They must appreciate their responsibilities as a civilized nation and be alive to the demands which will be placed upon them once they have become part of a modern community.

If an individual is to play his proper role in the building of a community of the peoples, he must be able to feel that he is part of a group which has become one during the course of history and is equipped with specific creative gifts – i.e. he must be able to feel loyalty to his own nation and its mission in civilization. All this leads me to believe that if the European unity which we desire is to be established, it will be necessary for the Germans to recover their sense of national identity. There was therefore good reason why, after the second world war, Germany's neighbours tended to regard the 'European idealism' of many Germans as an attempt to run away from their national dilemma. The impression got about that the German people were ashamed of being Germans and were trying to rid themselves of the burden of the recent past by seeking to dissolve their identity in the vast mass of a united Europe. Germany's Europe enthusiasts have unquestionably laid themselves open to the unspoken reproach that they have been trying to throw their national individuality into a melting pot by opting for integration in order thus to overcome their past.

Regardless of exactly how much justice there is in this view, the German people would do well to heed the warning that they must make up their minds where they wish to stand. Once they have succeeded in recovering their sense of national identity, they will be able to enter into a political partnership with the other peoples of Europe in a spirit of co-operation and desire for organic unity. Since the German people live in the centre of a Europe which is divided by power politics and ideological strife, they must not waste their efforts in a bid to restore their nation State. Even if success were theoretically possible, it could only be achieved subject to unsatisfactory limitations. In principle, however, such a restoration would neither be in accord with, nor would it promote, the general trend of developments. In any case, this restoration can only lie in some far distant future and, even if it could be achieved, could only be accomplished in conformity with conditions dictated by Moscow. Towards the end of the second world war and during the years immediately following, the USSR had its eye on the Rhine and the Atlantic; encouraged by certain American policies it may, at that time, have hoped for an early US withdrawal from Europe and regarded the continent, bleeding as it was from a thousand wounds, as easy prey. The USSR tried to get its foot into the Western door when it demanded a share in the control of the Rhine-Ruhr area and it did its utmost by way of ineffective threats and shock tactics to prevent the establishment of the Federal Republic and its entry into a military alliance with the West. But despite all these efforts it has had to abandon – for how long we do not know – its aim of creating a communist State embracing the whole of Germany. The German Federal Republic is the second most important economic Power in the West, though it is admittedly some considerable way behind the USA, while the Soviet Zone* is the second economic Power, after the USSR, among the members of the Eastern bloc. Together, the two would have a potential which – so Moscow believes – would disturb still further the already unstable equilibrium of the Eastern bloc. Even Ulbricht is occasionally regarded as a nuisance by his communist Protecting Power and his other allies; how much more would the German people's 'bad' qualities be feared – even if they were ruled by a German communist government – if the latter had at its disposal the potential of more than 70 million people and an area of 136,000 square miles, together with the continued and integrated economic resources of the two parts of Germany? What Moscow wants is a devoted, reliable and modest government in the 'German Democratic Republic' and an isolated, despised, internally weak, externally neutral and militarily powerless Federal Republic, whose economic resources would be made available to

*I.e. the 'German Democratic Republic – '.

94

the Kremlin by a Federal Government trembling before Moscow. All this is to be achieved, at the very latest, through the German peace treaty.

Nation States are an anachronism, particularly in the Europe of today, because of their inadequate area and population, and cannot function as viable units in international competition. This is why, in present-day conditions, a nation's determination to maintain itself must be reflected in its ability and willingness to leave behind the narrow notions of the past and to accept the need to refashion its existence so that it may meet the demands of the second technological revolution. It would not only be a waste of time but a threat to the wellbeing and continued existence of the peoples of Europe if they were to go on debating the outdated problems of the organization and reorganization of Central Europe's nation States. The German people's sense of national responsibility must therefore be reflected, not so much in a demand for political reunification – a demand which in present conditions is in any case not realistic, however desirable it may be from the human, and however well founded from the legal point of view – as in a political resolve to help bring about conditions in Europe which will guarantee the freedom, prosperity and economic and cultural vigour of future generations of the entire German people.

Once they realize that the nation State has become an outdated structure which can no longer safeguard the European peoples' ability to determine their own future, welfare and spiritual progress, it should be easier for the Germans to decide that it is in their national interest to help create a large territorial unit within which the German people will again be able to live as one. Those Germans who now live in the Federal Republic and enjoy much greater freedom to decide their own fate than the people of the 'German Democratic Republic' carry a correspondingly heavier burden of responsibility for the nation's future. This must be reflected in vigorous action to preserve and safeguard the essential values of the nation as a whole. To be able to remain Germans – in other words, to be able to carry over intact the foundations of our national identity into the era of space travel and to restore the unity of our people – we must become Europeans.

Not one of the peoples of Europe will be able to dispense with this process of rethinking if it is to remain capable of life and to continue as a cultural force. Since the institution of the nation State originally came into being by the will of the people, it can only be set aside by an act of the popular will. Though it may be possible carefully to co-ordinate the activities of States and peoples by means of supranational institutions created synthetically, such institutions will never be a driving force for political unity. To deny the nations the task of deciding of their own free will in favour of life within a greater unity for the sake of the common good would be to deny them their right to exist or, at the very least, it would be to fail totally to appreciate their historic significance.

However, the nations cannot simply be done away with, and even to attempt anything of the sort would be wrong. For our own comparatively small Europe has no greater asset at its disposal if it is to hold its own in competition with the World Powers than the diversity of its national talents, which have grown, each in its own soil, have become specialized and have attained great heights of achievement. However many examples the USA, that vast political and economic unit, may be able to furnish Europe in the way of concentration and rational use of resources, flexible management and efficient marketing, the old continent still retains qualities which must not be destroyed or tampered with if the European organism as a whole is not to fail.

However you may look at it, the diversity of its nations remains Europe's hallmark. These nations have lived side by side through the ages, at times in amity and at others in opposition, and during the course of their history have produced the spiritual and material foundations which remain valid for the whole of mankind and on which even tomorrow's world will have to rest. The nations of Europe, at any rate in the light of present-day knowledge, occupy a position of unequalled importance. If they were to undergo a kind of 'chemical' transformation in some melting pot, some process of standardization, this could only lead to a loss of vitality by these nations rather than to their desired rapid growth.

Hence, the peoples of Europe, aware of their fine traditions and husbanding their inherited skills, must grow into a community. What we have in mind in this context is a Europe of the nations, a Europe which, having overcome its former division into a multiplicity of States, has become a greater Fatherland. The notion of a family of nations, which presupposes that each of its members retains a degree of individuality, should be the guiding light for all efforts in Europe towards promoting co-operation and integration. Only a genuinely federal structure can do justice, within a united Europe, to the true significance of the nations.

In this connection, we must beware of two pitfalls. They are:

1. We must not succumb to the delusion that Europe will be able to forge its political unity as a result of the Common Market. Admittedly, the establishment of the Common Market following the failure of the European Defence Community, which was to have enabled the foreign and defence policies of the six member States (France, Germany, Italy, Belgium, Holland and Luxembourg) to be harmonized, was a correct, and indeed an essential, measure. However, this cannot take the place of a political decision to set up a European Federal State, although it can create the basis for such a decision.

2. It would be wrong to think that Europe can be created as a Power in its own right through a voluntary co-ordination of policies – particularly the foreign and defence policies of the Six – by setting up a kind of confederation under France's leadership but without creating federal institutions. It is no use thinking that a simple addition of the potentials of Europe's various nation States can take the place of the creation of a large, integrated area. This is just as true of the political-military as of the scientific-technological-industrial sphere. The USA would not be what it is today if it were merely a grouping of sovereign States. Even if a federal working partnership of six or more European countries were to be created, with each retaining unrestricted national sovereignty, it would be no use expecting such a traditional coalition, dominated by one Power, to maintain itself for any length of time. Internal changes in one country, external threats against, or temptations held out to, another would soon show up the instability of such a structure. In fact, it would be true to say that the very nature of such an organism – based as it would be on the rule of unanimity coupled with the freely accepted subordination of its members to one dominating Power – would be a standing challenge to outsiders to try to bring down this constellation by attempts to influence its internal affairs and by political manoeuvres. Such a structure would be neither sufficiently

credible nor strong enough to claim a real say in the counsels of the great.

Finally, let me say that a future European Power must be free from anti-American resentments and tendencies. On the contrary, once established as an important partner of the USA it would look to the latter for support and the Soviets would therefore not feel inclined to try to convert it into an ally of their own against America. There are important people in the USA, such as George Ball, who want such a European Power to be created for the sake of the United States itself. 'I would . . . like to see a strong assertive Europe, expressing its independent views and its own personality. I have little fear that over the years such a Europe would disagree with the United States on many great issues. . . . We would, I think, find ourselves working closely together . . . because we could regard one another for the first time with full mutual respect, recognizing that equality was now a fact and no longer a stylized figure of speech, which deceived no one – least of all the participants. . . . A united Europe can be our mature good friend, giving us from time to time sound advice, bringing to world councils its own insights, agreeing or disagreeing as the case may be, but acting always from the same larger purposes that it shares with us. . . .'

The emergence of a European Power allied to the USA as a political force which would be neither anti-American nor anti-Russian would make possible a considerable reduction in the strength of the American forces in Europe. In other words, backed by the alliance and with its own nuclear potential, such a Power could bring about an end to the confrontation between the USA and the USSR in Europe.

These ideas – or, as some may think, bitter home truths – are not meant to exclude the possibility of such a European Union pursuing a policy fashioned in accordance with the basic French concepts, with France playing the part of a *primus inter pares* during a transitional confederal phase and in the ensuing period. However, this would have to be done without rancour towards the USA, and provided the latter not only does not oppose the efforts at achieving European unity but actually supports them – to its own advantage. There would have to be an open door for Britain, with whom negotiations would have to be held regarding her entry into the Common Market, and there must be no isolated French approaches to Moscow.

The peoples of Europe, in view of the 'structural revolution' brought about by the advent of nuclear energy, electronics, supersonic flight, plastics and space travel, have no choice open to them other than to form a team if they wish to maintain themselves as cultural and industrial nations. The closer European co-operation can be made, the better chance there will be of the talents and qualities of the various nations being able to flourish and develop in an atmosphere of both competition and a pooling of ideas and skills. If this is done, the peoples will be able to devote themselves to cultivating the creative gifts they have acquired through tradition and inheritance. In this way, the nation will be preserved as the spiritual homeland of the peoples, while the political fatherland of the European community of peoples will be the Federal State they will set up and within which the determination of each nation to assert its specific identity will find scope for expression. Inevitably, the emotional and ideological content of what people, during the first half of this century, used to understand by the concepts of 'nation', 'fatherland' and 'homeland' will change profoundly.

Both the will to live of the various peoples and their spiritual unity, reflected in a sense of true solidarity, will be essential to the growth of a European awareness. In this context, the German situation, with its specific problems, is of particular importance. The Germans must play a key role in bringing the 'European family' together. A Europe which is to be a greater fatherland to the German people cannot end either at the Elbe or the Oder. One of its characteristics must be a 'European right of domicile' which will allow a German, just as members of any of the neighbouring peoples to the east, west, south or north, to take up residence and look for work as equal citizens in whatever part of Europe they choose. Only when they are able to live and work – should they so desire – where their fathers used to live and work, will its people recognize Europe as their fatherland. If a German nation State were established, it would be difficult to achieve this. However, in a 'Europe of the nations', brought together in peace, the freedom of movement of all citizens would be a natural concomitant of the prevailing legal system.

99

Europe no longer provides fertile ground for reactionary nationalism, despite the elaborate efforts which are still being made here and there to foster it and despite the fact that in some areas nationalist feelings are being aroused as a reaction to foreign domination. The nationalist tendencies which have emerged in Eastern and South-Eastern Europe must be considered to be of a reactive, rather than a reactionary, nature. In some of these countries, the populations should have been organized in multi-national rather than nation States in the first place; in others, the people have not yet succeeded in completing the historical process of national unification. The present nationalistic tendencies in certain parts of Eastern Europe are to some extent connected with the polycentric trends within communism; above all, however, they must be seen as a national reawakening of these peoples, eager to rid themselves of their unilateral dependence on the all-powerful USSR. The East Europeans should be the first to learn the lessons of history, and particularly of contemporary events, and realize that if the peoples and States of Europe rely each on their own devices, they will not be able to assert their rights and interests in the face of the World Powers. Although this realization may still only be dormant, it opens up the prospect that the present mood of nationalism in Eastern Europe will the more readily change into a sense of European solidarity the better we succeed in devising practical means of overcoming the present division of Europe. This, surely, must be the purpose of our efforts to bring about a relaxation of tension in Europe and of promoting an economic and cultural rapprochement between the States and peoples of Western and Eastern Europe.

The divided people of Germany, living as they are in the centre of all these events, will only be able to fulfil their national mission on behalf of Europe if they succeed in preserving their spiritual unity and resolve to act as one. In the present state of Germany's political partition, it is therefore our task to use every means available to us to foster the German national consciousness, with the aim of strengthening European solidarity at the same time. Moscow is seeking to deepen the division of Europe for its own imperialistic ends, which it presents to the world in an ideological guise. Within its German sphere of influence, it is seeking to make use, in this connection, of separatist tendencies. Unless we succeed in foiling this Soviet attempt at breaking the German people's national unity and unless we gain support for our own cause, it will be difficult to ensure the success of this cause of ours, the cause of all-European unity, which, once achieved, will enable the German people to come together again.

The population of the 'German Democratic Republic' – so we are being told more and more often – have long since developed a 'sense of statehood'. They are now said to be ready to accept as permanent the structure put together by the Party, nowadays usually referred to here shamefacedly as 'the other part of Germany'. Much of the talk which one hears on either side of the demarcation line may seem to confirm this impression. However, it is bound to be difficult to determine accurately, during the odd visit to Central Germany, whether this 'recognition' is being accorded by the people to the communist system from conviction or resignation. In other words, do we have to depend on speculation or, at best, on scant evidence, insufficient to allow any valid conclusions to be drawn?

This question, which is of crucial importance to the Federal Republic, is not as difficult to answer as most people think. The Pankow regime has itself furnished us with ample evidence to show that there is in fact no 'sense of statehood' among the people whom it governs. If Walter Ulbricht and his officials were really able to depend on the people over whom they hold sway they would have no need to treat their 'citizens' as subjects and to rule them with brute force. Unlike Poland, Czechoslovakia, Hungary, Rumania and Bulgaria, the 'German Democratic Republic' looks every bit like a monument to Stalin left standing in the heart of Europe. This alone shows that the people who have to live in the 'GDR' have not ceased to resist. In other words, the East Berlin regime is not recognized by the majority of its own subjects. This is clear for instance, from the instructions which have been issued to hold the 'National People's Army' in check. Thus, some time ago, an order was issued to the commanding officers of the border troops. The idea was to restrict still further the soldiers' chances of deserting from the 'National People's Army'. The order states that duty rosters and postings must be kept secret. No soldier is to know in advance what his duties are to be during the next few hours. The precise duties of frontier patrols must be kept secret up to within one hour of the beginning of a given assignment. When troops are ferried to frontier areas, it is forbidden to remove truck covers in order to prevent members of the 'National People's Army' memorizing the route. A strict watch is kept on troops on leave.

What sort of an army is it which has to take such steps to prevent desertions? The young men who wear the uniform of the 'National People's Army' belong to a generation which has never known anything but the 'German Democratic Republic'. Even as children they were fed a diet of lying propaganda, and they had to go through a process of membership, first of the 'Young Pioneers', then the 'Free German Youth' and finally the 'Society for Sport and Technology', in order to serve 'Germany's only State of the workers and peasants'. As for the schools, they do their best to exalt the 'socialist gains' of the 'GDR' and urge the people to give these 'achievements' their love and protection. But none of this has evidently been enough to arouse a 'sense of statehood' among the people, so that brute force is to this day needed to make the army obey its orders.

It should be borne in mind, moreover, that the frontier troops have repeatedly been 'purged' so as to make them an 'élite of loyalty to communism'. But the fact that the top command of the 'National People's Army' is still worried lest its soldiers run away – despite the presence of mine belts and the practice of shooting on sight – goes to show how doubtful is the stability of the 'State' between the Elbe and the Oder. It owes its existence solely to Moscow and would collapse like a house of cards if it really depended on the support of the people it is supposed to represent. To accord international recognition to the 'GDR' would be to disregard these facts. The people who live there would not only derive no benefit from such a recognition; they would be bound to regard it as a betrayal.

It will be our task to ensure that the people who live in the other part of Germany retain their will to live. As for ourselves, we shall never be able to bring ourselves to regard that part of our country as foreign territory, and it is our wish that we may be reunited with it under the roof of a greater European fatherland. It is the spirit of European solidarity which must hold the German nation together; it is that spirit which alone should guide us in all the political decisions we must make in the all-German context. Like the other peoples of this continent, the entire German people now faces a great test. It is important that the German people should realize the gravity of the errors and crimes that have been committed in the past, but this can only be done given a normal, sober and rational attitude to the tasks of the present and the future. National megalomania in any shape or form would be just as detrimental as morbid complexes about the past. The evil that has been committed in the past cannot be overcome so long as the nation feels that the problems it will have to face in the future are beyond its powers. A nation lives by the knowledge that it has a mission to fulfil, and it can discover this mission only if it is given a chance of playing a creative part in the shaping of a new world order of up-to-date dimensions.

# 8 *Germany – a European Problem*

If we want to make sure that the future is ours and that the Germans will be able to fulfil themselves in the Europe of tomorrow, we must tackle the problem of reunification differently. To be able to do this, we must be clear about our priorities. The first step must be a union of free European countries as a preliminary step leading to a greater federation in which all Germans would be able to live in freedom. German reunification will become a fact only if Western Europe's progress is such that it becomes a focus of attraction for the countries of Eastern Europe. The fear the smaller member States of the Eastern bloc have of the threat of German 'revanchism' will vanish to the extent to which we succeed in forging the political unity of Western Europe. Relations between the two halves of the old continent will then develop so strongly that Ulbricht's regime will come to seem a survival from a forgotten age.

It follows that if we are to ensure the continued existence of our people, the same principle must apply to us as holds good for our neighbours to the West and East: we shall only be able to remain Germans if we become Europeans. There is therefore only one way in which we, who live in the Federal Republic, can interpret our duty to fight for the fundamental rights of the entire German people. We must work for the maintenance and strengthening of Europe's resolve to achieve its unity and press for a resumption of the efforts to integrate Europe. The very fact that we are free to decide our own domestic and external policies places a responsibility for the fate of all Germans upon those of us who live in the free part of Germany. This freedom gives our Government, which has an authentic mandate from the electors, both the right and the duty to take such measures as are necessary to safeguard the existence of the entire people. Thus we must vigorously press the view that our fellow countrymen on the other side of the Elbe are entitled to the right of self-determination. But we must not delude ourselves that there can be any genuine self-determination for our own and the other European peoples unless they win the right to play a joint role in the processes of decision-making on a world scale.

In all the discussions about reunification, the idea must never be allowed to take hold that Germany might conceivably be pre-vailed upon to renounce her right to self-determination. We ought to be ready and willing to drop Germany's demands regarding State sovereignty and work for our aspirations as members of a European Federation. In no case, however, are we prepared to give up our national rights and demands as human beings by agreeing to a perpetuation of the present partition of our country and of the status quo. It is up to us Europeans to construct a European edifice into which a reunified Germany can be absorbed as a full member without having to renounce any of her inalienable rights.

Some may object that by drawing attention to these rights I am blocking a possible deal with Moscow whereby the latter would let go of Central Germany in return for an offer of concessions in the field of security. Those who believe that such a deal is possible should bear in mind, however, how valuable the 'GDR' is to the Kremlin in view of present circumstances and the Kremlin's current views.

As for the importance of the Soviet Zone within the military system of the Warsaw Pact, this is evident from its geographic position alone. The area in which our fellow countrymen are being oppressed by the 'Socialist Unity Party of Germany' juts out like a promontory into Western territory. It can be used both as a for-ward bastion for the defence of the USSR and as a springboard for aggression against free Europe. Although such an attack is unlikely for the time being, it could happen if the deterrent power of the North Atlantic Pact should fail.

A Soviet offensive based on Central Germany could be waged in four directions. From the north towards Schleswig-Holstein and Jutland, in order to give the Soviet Union control over our access routes to the Baltic; along either side of the Helmstedt autobahn, with a view to occupying the Ruhr; from the Thuringian Forest in the direction of the Rhine-Main triangle centred on Frankfurt; and from the border area between Czechoslovakia and the Soviet Zone, in the direction of Nuremberg and Munich. Thanks to its control over Central Germany, the East would thus have considerable advantages in a war of aggression against the West.

The Soviet Zone's importance to the USSR also stems from its industrial potential. The so-called 'German Democratic Republic' is technically further advanced than either Czechoslovakia or Poland, and supplies the USSR mainly with machinery and materials for its rearmament. 'GDR' exports of this type to Russia greatly exceed those of the other member States of the 'Council for Mutual Economic Aid' – while 'GDR' imports from the USSR largely consist of goods which the Pankow regime requires for the production of the supplies needed by Moscow. These deliveries and services are included annually in advance as 'firm commitments' in the economic plans of the Soviet Union and therefore determine the target figures which the 'Socialist Unity Party' imposes on the factories and workers in the Soviet Zone.

The Soviet Zone's output of actual armaments is rather modest. It produces, in the main, infantry weapons and other simple military equipment, while Poland and Czechoslovakia produce tanks and guns on a considerable scale, mostly under Soviet licence. Although uranium ore is being mined by German enterprises at Aue and Ronneburg, the production of fissionable materials in the Soviet Zone is not permitted, and the raw materials for nuclear weapons extracted in Germany are earmarked exclusively for export to Russia.

The Soviet Zone's human potential is also an important military factor from the USSR's point of view. In the spring of 1965, Army General Karl Heinz Hoffmann, the Ulbricht regime's Defence Minister, proclaimed proudly that the 'National People's Army' had become part of the Warsaw Pact's 'first strategic echelon'. It therefore seems that the General Staff in Moscow now considers Pankow's troops worthy and capable of operating side by side with the units of Warsaw, Prague and the Red Army itself. The time thus seems to be over when the 'National People's Army' was relegated to the second rank. Its progress in the strategic rankings amounts in practice to a Soviet version of the call 'Germans, to the front!'

Signs pointing that way began to appear as long ago as 1963, since when large units of the Soviet Zone Army have been taking part with increasing frequency in joint exercises of the Warsaw Pact armies. Naval exercises in the Baltic in which, in addition to Soviet and Polish, German squadrons took part, have shown that the Navy is not behind the naval forces of the other satellites as regards training and equipment. The same is presumably true of the Air Force.

The fact that the Soviets think fairly highly of the efficiency of the 'National People's Army' – which is estimated to have some two hundred thousand men – is also evident from the following: For some time now, Moscow has been treating the supply of modern weapons and equipment to Pankow as a priority task. It may be thought striking, in this connection, that at its various parades last year, and also during its last manoeuvres, the 'National People's Army' displayed tactical rockets capable of carrying nuclear warheads. The missiles concerned are known by the NATO code name 'Frog' (range about forty miles) and 'Scud' (range about a hundred and sixty miles). The Soviet occupation troops have control over the nuclear warheads, but the fact that the 'People's Army' is equipped with missiles shows how eager the Kremlin is to give recognition to Pankow's military forces.

It is thus clear that the USSR feels that it has its German satellites and their army on a tight rein. Naturally, Moscow is hardly likely to have much confidence in the 'People's Army' troops' loyalty to communism. However, the highly sophisticated system of surveillance which the 'Socialist Unity Party' regime – backed by the four hundred thousand Soviet troops stationed in Central Germany – maintains in order to keep a watch on its soldiers, is sufficient guarantee in the eyes of the Kremlin that these troops would march if they were ordered to do so. None of this means that the 'GDR', which, in the political sense, functions as a clamp which holds the entire rickety edifice of the Eastern bloc together, has become an equal partner of the USSR in the military sense. Nevertheless, it may be considered a useful and important instrument of Soviet strategy. Since the political stability of this

State, which exists by the grace of Moscow, is essential if that instrument is to function, it is clear that the Kremlin must be interested in seeing the harsh practices of its Pankow branch continue provided they do not give rise to serious trouble. The fact is that these methods guarantee the reliability of the Soviet Zone; any psychological disadvantages which Russia may have to put up with as a result of the continued existence of the tyrannical regime in Central Germany are considered by her to be of minor importance, especially since the 'Socialist Unity Party' dictatorship is regarded by most people in the West as a German institution and only by a handful as a regime imposed by the Russians.

In view of the overriding strategic importance which the country now oppressed by Pankow has in Moscow's eyes, is there any chance in the foreseeable future of our being able to 'buy out' the Soviet Zone. Can the USSR be persuaded to loosen its hold on this German jewel in the Red Tsars' crown, let alone to run the risk that it may drop out of its communist setting altogether? How heavy a 'price' would have to be paid? What sort of an offer would have to be made to persuade the USSR that it stood to gain not only the equivalent of the 'GDR' but even to make a profit?

Anyone who is prepared to look at this proposition carefully will have to agree that the Federal Republic – and with it the whole of continental Europe – would have to make concessions in terms of security which, though they might result in a minimal relaxation of the stranglehold exercised by Pankow would, in the long run, give Moscow a chance of incorporating the whole of Germany in its empire. A policy liable to bring about such a situation would certainly not advance the cause of our country's unity and freedom. Those who call for 'substantial initiatives with a view to reunification' would do well to remember this. There is no point in ignoring the hard military realities with which we are faced. Above all, in devising our policies, we must not overlook the fact that Russia has always treated military considerations as of decisive importance. This was true of Russian military policies for many centuries before 1917, and it has remained true ever since. All that has changed is that the imperial-military considerations of old have now been supplemented by an ideological-revolutionary aspect, of particular importance in the case of Germany. We must be careful, therefore, not to fall victim to illusions liable to tempt us into dangerous adventures.

Despite the boorish tone which Moscow continues to consider appropriate in its propaganda against Bonn, the view is gaining ground in our country that, in the final analysis, the Soviet Union means no harm to the Federal Republic and has no intention whatever of incorporating it in its power sphere. The Kremlin, it is said, has enough trouble dealing with its difficulties in the 'socialist camp' and, of all things, wants a reunification of Germany under the aegis of communism least of all, since this would present the USSR with insuperable problems. On the other hand, in order to safeguard our own peace and freedom, we would have to recognize the 'GDR' as an independent State. Moreover, it would be up to us to prove by as complete a measure of disarmament as possible that we are serious about renunciation of the use of force.

Let us assume, by all means, that for the present the Soviet leaders are not interested in seeing a Red German Reich established because in the event the USSR might find that it had bitten off more than it could swallow. I have pointed this out in earlier passages. But in the long run, Bonn cannot rely blindly on the Soviet Union allowing itself to be guided by this consideration alone should the chance occur one day of rounding off the Soviet empire without too much danger by adding the Federal Republic to it. Many a person has wolfed down a festive goose without hesitation, knowing full well that he would eventually get indigestion, because at the time he could not resist the tempting odour wafting in from the kitchen. Man does not always act reasonably, nor does he always keep within rational bounds. Moscow, too, has its hawks and doves, and there is a school of thought there which considers that the complete political paralysis, conquest or, if necessary, the destruction of the Federal Republic may one day become an inescapable political necessity.

According to certain clever analysts of Pankow's policies, it is the basic concept of the Ulbricht regime to outbid, with the USSR's backing, Bonn's claim to be the sole spokesman for the whole of Germany. The people who have to live under the rule of the 'Socialist Unity Party' are thus to be made to feel that theirs is the 'real fatherland' and that it is therefore their task to work for the 'liberation' of the territory governed from Bonn. In other words, we are confronted with the converse of the 'roll-back' doctrine once proclaimed by Washington against Moscow.

The dialectical logic of the communist programme emerges very clearly from a speech made in the spring of 1967 by Professor Albert Norden, the propaganda chief of the 'Socialist Unity Party'. He declared:

The problem of the German nation is, first and foremost, a class problem. To try to unite socialism and monopoly capitalism would be a betrayal of peace, a betrayal of socialism, a betrayal of the people and nation. Monopoly capitalism is out to serve its own interests alone at the expense of those of the people. The socialist aims of the working class, on the other hand, are intended to benefit the people as a whole and must be fought for and attained by the people as a whole. This is why the building of socialism in the German Democratic Republic amounts to the pursuit of a German national policy in practice. Since only socialism can offer the German people a secure social, political and national future, only socialism can be the solution – for West Germany, too. . .

Thus, if Pankow now seems to be on the defensive and trying to achieve nothing more than a stabilization of its position of power, it is pursuing these tactics with the sole object of achieving a position from which it intends eventually to deploy its forces for attack. Therefore, nothing could be more useful to the 'Socialist Unity Party' than an international recognition of its 'German Democratic Republic'. Once Walter Ulbricht and his comrades had got the world to confirm the 'legitimacy' of the regime in Central Germany, they would have a very real chance of concentrating all their energies on expansion. Bonn would therefore be most ill-advised to follow the promptings of those who are pressing it to 'recognize the reality of the other German State'. If that advice were taken this would not result – as many seem to think – in a 'relaxation' of tension. On the contrary, new tensions would arise as a result of the other side's aggressive activities. I agree with George Ball, who said: 'I see no chance that the Soviet Union would ever agree to reunification until there was a fundamental change in the structure of Europe. To accept reunification under today's conditions would mean that Moscow must relinquish control over its principal satellite and thus precipitate the dissolution of the Warsaw Pact system.'

In this connection, I should like to discuss Poland's position – often misjudged – within the Warsaw Pact.

In my view, it is a mistake to think that a recognition of the Oder-Neisse line as Germany's eastern frontier would encourage Poland, and might even enable her first to loosen and then to shake off altogether the bonds which tie her to Moscow, to rid herself of the shackles imposed on her by her defence policy and to regain her freedom of action in foreign affairs. This view is based on the erroneous assumption that Warsaw's loyalty to Moscow – and Pankow – is essentially a result of the Soviet Union's guarantee of Poland's so-called western frontier.

In actual fact, this is not the main reason why Poland has to remain on the Soviet side. The real reason is that she is one of the strategically most important areas within Russia's European sphere of influence. Warsaw is simply in no position to steer a political course which would permit it to extricate itself from its enforced alliance with Moscow. Any such attempt would expose the Polish People's Republic to the same ruthless treatment as was suffered by Hungary in 1956 and a sound beating at the hands of her powerful neighbour. The Polish people, who by virtue of their culture and traditional sympathies undoubtedly feel themselves greatly attracted to the West, will therefore remain prisoners of the USSR in the political and military sense, despite the fact that they may gradually be given wider opportunities for what has come to be called 'liberalization' than are enjoyed by the so-called 'German Democratic Republic'. Gomulka's regime is well aware of this situation, from which it cannot escape in view of the superior power of the Soviet Union. Therefore, even if it felt so inclined, it cannot risk arousing the suspicion that it might one day wish to break out of the East's treaty system or to 'betray' Pankow to the West.

Consequently, there can be no changes in this respect under present circumstances. No tactics, however clever and flexible, will succeed in diminishing to any extent the USSR's military interest in the Polish People's Republic, and it is this interest which dictates Warsaw's attitude. The manpower potential which Poland represents from the viewpoint of the Soviet military machine is also of considerable significance. With a population of 31 million, Poland has 380,000 regular troops and 2,600,000 trained reserves and can thus claim to have the biggest non-Soviet army among the Powers of the Eastern bloc. It is unlikely that the Kremlin could easily be persuaded to let go of these troops, which would be at its disposal in the event of war. And there is no doubt that it might lose these troops if it were to allow Warsaw a chance of flirting with the West and indulging in intrigues against Pankow.

But, important though they are to Moscow, it is not because of the Polish armed forces that the former is imposing tighter political control on Warsaw than, for example, on Bucharest, Budapest, Sofia and Prague. As distinct from the South-East European satellites of the USSR, who are allowed to profit from their peripheral position, Poland must bear in mind that she is of crucial importance to the Soviet Union's strategy, for she forms the link between Russia and Central Germany. If it were not able to place complete reliance on the Polish People's Republic, the USSR would be unable to give the 'GDR' the sort of power-political backing which the latter needs in order properly to administer the Red Army's German area of deployment in accordance with the requirements of Soviet foreign policy.

Poland would come to occupy an even more important place in the plans of the Soviet Union if the Kremlin were to make a start with the execution of the necessary technical preparations for a nuclear and conventional 'disengagement' in Central Europe. The USSR needs all the Polish territory, its entire width and depth, in order to be able rapidly to return to their original locations any nuclear weapons or troops that might have been brought home to encourage the West to take parallel measures by way of thinning out its military cover. For all supplies – troops, arms, ammunition, military equipment and all other materials – must be carried from East to West, be it by road, rail, sea or air, across Gomulka's People's Republic. These lines of communication have been considerably improved and expanded during the last few years. In addition, an oil pipeline from Mozyr in Byelorussia via Plock in Poland to Schwedt-on-the-Oder in Germany is to be completed shortly.

A moving apart of the power blocs, an idea which many politicians in the West still find fascinating, has therefore never offered any hope of a loosening of the Soviet military hold on Poland but has, on the contrary, always been bound to lead to its tightening. The fact that the opposite view has been widely accepted may be due to Moscow's skill in having all its plans for partially demilitarized zones in Europe presented by Warsaw; this has made them seem more credible and thus more effective.

To sum up my thoughts regarding a 'rational' solution of the German problem: Germany's reunification can be achieved neither by force nor by accepting the Soviet conditions. Any attempt to use force would lead to reunification in a cemetery; on the other hand, to accept the Soviet conditions would mean that we should all find ourselves reunified in a communal prison. The Soviets are still basing their action on the hypothesis of a possible confederation of the two German States – i.e. a confederation between Bonn and Pankow. This would include a 'Free City of West Berlin', with each State preserving its present social order. The Federal Republic would have to submit to complete neutralization and far-reaching demilitarization and would only be permitted to keep a police force for the maintenance of internal law and order.

According to Moscow's concept, the Soviet-occupied zone would have to submit to the same conditions. However, in its case the effects would be quite different. While the Federal Republic would find itself in a vacuum, the communist part of Germany would retain its extremely close links with the Eastern bloc by virtue of its internal structure, its international links with the communist parties, its strategy, ideology and geographical situation. The American and British troops would probably have to leave the Continent of Europe, while the Soviet troops would only withdraw a distance of a few hundred miles and would be in a position to return at any time on some pretext or other.

Another element in Moscow's concept of a 'confederation of the two German States' is the establishment of joint institutions on a basis of equality, with the Federal Republic and the 'GDR' each providing half the delegates or members. There could be no better way to destroy Europe's unity, break up the Western alliance and draw the Federal Republic into the Soviet sphere of influence. This proposal is therefore unacceptable.

The fact is that no 'key to reunification' is to be found either in Moscow, Warsaw or Pankow. This can be proved by means of the following, admittedly somewhat far-fetched, hypothesis. Let us assume that Germany saw fit to make the following offer forthwith: The German Federal Republic will leave the Atlantic Alliance and the EEC; accept the Rapacki Plan and permanent denuclearization; reduce the strength of the Bundeswehr to a hundred thousand men; guarantee for a period of a hundred years Germany's demilitarization and neutralization under international control; and make available to the Soviet Union a sum of DM100,000 to 120,000 million over a period of twenty years as investment aid in order to help make good the war damage sustained by the USSR. And now, to continue, I shall go one step further. The German Federal Republic promises, for the remainder of the twentieth century, not to put up the question of reunification for discussion. If, in return for all this, Germany were to demand a single concession, to wit, that the Soviet Zone should be given the status enjoyed by Austria – full freedom to decide its internal order and social system, i.e. free, secret elections – if we were to make such an offer, I am convinced that the Soviet reply would either be a straight-forward *nyet* or possibly a more roundabout formula, such as: First you carry out in full your side of the bargain, and when you have done so we shall find it easier to discuss the last point.

This extreme hypothesis is not as far-fetched as it may seem; a somewhat less extreme version was recently put up for discussion by the Hudson Institute of New York.

Under the terms of this latter proposal, Germany would sign a 'peace treaty' leaving her divided into two States for a period of twenty years. The two States would have to undertake to abandon all their existing alliances and to join no new ones, not to acquire any nuclear weapons, not to press for any territorial changes and not to permit any movements of refugees from one State to the other. ... The security of the two German States would be guaranteed by the former enemies of the Reich, who, moreover, would have to evacuate all foreign troops from the areas on either side of the demarcation line within a period of three years. On the other hand, both States would be permitted conventional forces – twenty divisions in the case of the Federal Republic and ten in that of the 'German Democratic Republic'. The four sectors of Berlin would be amalgamated into a 'Free City' under international control and the Oder-Neisse line would have to be recognized as the Western frontier of the Polish People's Republic. Only after two decades would the three Germanies, whose existence would thus have been confirmed, be permitted to unite in a single State, freely to sign any treaty and to acquire all types of arms. The question of the rights and liberties of the citizens of the 'Free City' of Berlin and the 'German Democratic Republic' is left open.

Anyone who soberly examines this blueprint of a peace treaty must be amazed, nay frightened, at this notion of a dynamic nation – and thus, in the last analysis, the whole of Europe – being 'frozen' in its present state of political development. Any attempt to neutralize Central Europe could soon have the most dangerous consequences – it could lead to dissatisfaction, to turmoil and an explosion. George Ball was right in saying:

This approach to the German problem is not new. It was tried at Versailles in 1919 with disastrous results. It is a solution calculated to produce instability, demagoguery and frustration at the dangerous center of Europe. Both Europe and Germany deserve something more hopeful than the repetition of a discreditable past. . . . I am firmly convinced that there is no possibility for a long-range and stable European settlement unless we can find a solution that takes account of the interests of the German people, that permits them to play a role of substantial equality in Europe – a role both self-respecting and satisfying – and that enables them to direct their energies and talents to constructive ends.

The notion that unsolved problems can be rendered innocuous by simply 'freezing' them has evidently not yet been sufficiently dispelled either by the Korean War or the conflict in Vietnam. . . . But this must not be allowed to discourage us; on the contrary, we should regard it as a challenge and issue warning after warning even if we do get on the nerves of some of our allies, who may honestly think that their intentions towards us are well-meaning.

The ideas I have described are not based on a realistic assessment of Soviet policies. They may make the Kremlin smile, but they will never make it believe that they are to be taken seriously.

E

For all such Western notions fail to take account of the fact that the Kremlin cannot tolerate the restoration of normal civic rights and liberties, of which the people of this area have been deprived since 1933. The Kremlin cannot allow this to happen, if for no other reason than that it must assume that these people, despite, or perhaps precisely because of, the lessons they have received during their thirty-five years of life under a dictatorship would never vote for a communist system in a genuinely free and secret ballot. On the other hand, if such were the outcome, it would mean the collapse of the ideological edifice of communism and the doctrine of the inexorable march of human history towards communism would have been proved false. There would be no stopping the flood then; the dams would burst. What Soviet leadership could conceivably contemplate such a turn of events? It is time, therefore, that people stopped crediting the leaders in the Kremlin with ideas, sentiments and moral values which are peculiar to the West and ceased to judge these leaders and to assess their intentions by such yardsticks. There is no political surgery which can transplant people's hearts and minds at will!

In the final analysis, such ideas derive from a further error, which is particularly widespread in our own country – the notion that reunification can be achieved by means of national policies and along purely national lines. As against this, I should like to place on record my own view: I do not believe in the restoration of a German nation State. The German problem can only be solved within the framework of a united Europe.

Germany needs this united Europe more than any other country. After the war, uncertain of herself and abandoned by all, she looked to the European ideal as a way, not only of overcoming her recent past but as an honourable solution which would not give rise to concern among her neighbours and would enable her to turn her vast energies to good use. By contributing to the establishment of a European federation, Germany hoped to discover a new self.

This 'Europeanization of the German problem' requires, of course, that the German people's demand for the freedom of their divided country be unreservedly taken up and advocated by the West European community. We are thus faced with the task of creating political ties with Western Europe which will make it possible to treat the German problem, not as the national demand of one State but as a common European concern, for the partition of Germany is part and parcel of the division of Europe. Our Western partners must see that the seventeen million Germans who still live separated from us under communist domination share the fate of the other countries of Eastern Europe. We Germans must beware, therefore, of making our partitioned country and the fate of our brothers who have been separated from us into a special 'case'. A solution of the German problem can only be achieved as part of a general European settlement. This is no easy task. However, in her own interest, Germany must reconcile herself to the fact that the way ahead will be long, but it offers the only realistic hope. In any case, no one has been able to demonstrate convincingly that there is a shorter path.

The Federal Republic must therefore be prepared to enter into a European Confederation even if the latter should, in the first phase, not include the whole of Germany. Such a framework will offer the best guarantee that the new Europe will not be handicapped by unco-ordinated nationalistic or militaristic policies. The legitimate desire of the German people for unity within the framework of an all-European reunification must become part and parcel of European policy. In this way, the fear of a remilitarized and aggressive Germany will be eliminated.

A European policy designed to promote the growing together of Eastern and Western Europe in liberty, which did not at the same time honour the duty of pressing for the reunification of a people two thirds of whose members live in Western Europe and the remaining third in a country which belongs to the Moscow-dominated Warsaw Pact, would be unthinkable. A reunified Germany, recreated as a nation State pure and simple and comprising exclusively the present Federal Republic and the Soviet-occupied Zone, would give rise to an economic and political problem for the world the gravity of which cannot be overlooked. Such a unit would admittedly not be as strong as the United States of America or the Soviet Union; nevertheless, in terms of population and economic potential it would be more powerful than any other European country – larger than Britain, France or Italy. Notwithstanding the fact that these countries have given verbal assurances of support for Germany's reunification, it would be unrealistic not to see that the vision of a reunified Germany tied to no one and possessing such political, economic, and possibly also military, strength must worry these countries considerably. Nothing is said officially about this aspect of the problem, but we should do well not to delude ourselves and not to overlook this feeling of disquiet. 'If we are honest with ourselves', says George Ball, 'we must recognize that none of Germany's neighbours, East or West, is prepared to accept the emergence in the heart of Europe of an overshadowing nation of eighty million – at least without hedging the Germans about with such humiliating restrictions and discriminatory commitments as to assure trouble in the future.'

Right after the foundation of Bismarck's Reich in 1871, Germany was already faced with the task of reconciling her neighbours to the unaccustomed fact of her existence. Today it is even more necessary than it was then to create conditions for a reunification of Germany which will allay the resentment, suspicion or, worse still, the hostility of Germany's neighbours to the East and West. This is yet another reason why a reunified Germany must be integrated in a European framework. Only if this is done will she not be considered a political or military threat. But if a reunified Germany joins a European Federation – whose policy will naturally not be determined by her alone – and if Germany is not left in a political vacuum, there will be no possible chance of her being able to play off East and West against one another.

People should not continually overlook the fact that the problem of the existence of a German Reich between East and West has not been with us since yesterday. As I have said, Bismarck's smaller Germany was created during the final third of the nineteenth century. Bismarck fought tooth and nail, using all the resources of his diplomatic skill, exploiting every opening and occasionally resorting to blood and iron, to get the Reich' unwilling neighbours to agree to its creation. He knew that its neighbours – France, Russia and Austria – wanted to prevent the creation of a Middle Kingdom because it would threaten to disturb and distort the balance of power established by the Congress of Vienna. The peripheral Powers were bent on preventing the emergence of a new European centre of gravity in their midst. In so doing they were following their power-political instincts. Prussia was a country ruled by a dynasty, and, in view of her strategic position, military value and dependence on foreign alliances, was an esteemed and popular – if not a greatly loved – partner. However, a German Reich led by Prussia but with a potential far greater than Prussia's gave rise to extreme fears that its existence and political objectives might disturb the balance of power. Germany's only chance of getting off this particular line – the end of which was reached with the first world war – would have been either a reconciliation with France, friendship with Britain by giving up the quest for naval glory and global ambitions, or, finally, careful cultivation of the policy of reinsurance vis-à-vis Russia (and avoiding dangerous treaty obligations towards Austria-Hungary).

The need to reconcile the peripheral Powers with the fact of Germany's existence is just as much in evidence today as it was then. Germany's partition is a result of the policy pursued by Hitler, the Yalta decisions and the West's short-sightedness after the second world war. When Britain and America entered the war against Germany, they declared that it was their intention not only to free Europe from Hitler but to ensure the triumph of freedom, humanity and justice throughout the world – in Germany, Italy, Japan and wherever else these fundamental rights might have been violated. In regard to communism, however, it has not been implemented and the task remains, in equity, to be fulfilled. For Poland, Czechoslovakia, Hungary and the other European countries behind the Iron Curtain are just as much members of the European family as the countries of Western Europe. We must therefore think in terms of a united and free Europe and not just of a united Germany. We Germans must learn to look upon the question of our unity not as a national, but as an international, problem. Such an approach, admittedly, cannot bring a quick solution, but at least it is based on solid historical fact, on an examination of the internal changes in the communist camp and, last but not least, on an assessment of the Soviet Union's strategic situation between Red China and Europe.

Although limited bilateral German-Soviet negotiations could possibly lead to an easier atmosphere, they undoubtedly could not solve the complex problem with which we have to deal. This is why our European allies, backed by the United States, must negotiate on behalf of Germany and the whole of Europe. French and British diplomacy has greater scope in Eastern Europe and enjoys better credit there than does German diplomacy. The reasons for this are obvious. They are part of our tragic past. Our European allies may be able to convince our East European neighbours that the new Europe, far from being expansionist, will tie up the German potential and free the Soviets of the military burden of having to control and dominate territories whose peoples wish to live neither under Soviet nor under German rule.

After the first world war, the Western allies created the so-called *cordon sanitaire* – a buffer zone which was to keep Germany under control. The *cordon sanitaire* failed to meet its purpose. It was unable to do so the moment Germany became a strong military Power again, animated by nationalistic and expansionist aims. The region of the *cordon sanitaire* was torn hither and thither between Russia and Germany. After the second world war, Stalin turned the *cordon sanitaire* into a *cordon Stalinaire* by exploiting these old concepts for his own ends. It must now be our task to create, as a start, a buffer zone between Russia and Western Europe – an 'intermediate Europe' which will be dominated neither by the USSR nor by Western Europe. In the immediate future, this area will not be able to become part of a European community. It could, however, offer a satisfactory military guarantee to the Soviet Union once Germany and Western Europe have amalgamated.

In the long run, the Soviet Union might agree to the idea of an autonomous Europe. The existence of this new neighbour, which, though allied to the United States would not be under the latter's military control, would be in full accord with the Soviet Union's military security requirements, assuming always that it is the sole concern of the USSR to live in peace with Europe.

However, if we continue to act as we have done hitherto, indulging in the making of fine-sounding declarations about Germany and the drawing up of schemes for a future reunified Fatherland – with perhaps a conference about the German problem thrown in every other year – then all our efforts will be in vain. We must, once and for all, discard the old German-nationalist ideas of old, which unfortunately can still be encountered here and there. We must create the political realities of tomorrow – a new,

politically united Europe which, though not separated from the
United States, with which it will be linked by having a similar
order of society, will be able to stand on its own feet. We must,
at long last, start devising a policy for the future, a policy for
Europe!

# 9 *The Science and Technology Gap*

The unity of Western Europe is a worthwhile objective not only because of its importance to us if we are to reach our eventual goal – the unification of the whole of Europe – but for its own sake. Our continent is threatening to degenerate, both in political and economic terms, into an underdeveloped area. This will happen if the European States do not decide to go beyond their present more or less loose co-operation and to amalgamate their national potentials. Without this there can be no genuine self-determination. At best, Europe will have a modest share in the privilege of decision-making. In his book *The American Challenge*, which has not become a best-seller for nothing, the French author Jean-Jacques Servan-Schreiber pointed out this need and clearly defined the reasons for it. On the face of it, the title of his work might seem anti-American. However, it is not intended as a moral judgement, and even less as a criticism of American policies in Europe. The latter are not interpreted as a challenge in the sense of a provocation but as a challenge in the sense defined by Toynbee in his historical essays. Europe is faced with a 'challenge', a summons, a call, he says, and must find a 'response'. 'Challenge' and 'response' – the call of destiny and the ability to meet it – this is what determines the fate of civilizations. Whoever fails to answer this call is doomed to disappear as an independent factor. No matter what you may think of Servan-Schreiber's book – which first appeared in the summer of 1968, has been translated into many languages and has been well received in the USA also – no matter whether you consider individual statements in it to be misconceived or exaggerated, fundamentally it is the right sort of appeal on behalf of the right cause, made at the eleventh hour.

Europe is not concerned to recover her former position and to become the centre of the world again; the wheel of history has turned too far for that. No, Europe's real problem is to decide whether she is to be able, in the world of tomorrow, to stand up for herself as an independent entity or whether she is to become a 'satellite' of the United States. The latter would then be superior to Europe, not only in raw materials – which is of minor importance – but in ideas, planning, organizing ability, management, social vitality, size and population. The United States would surpass Europe by virtue of the advanced nature of her educational system, her economic and financial potential and, in general, by the scope of her activities in all the spheres decisive for the future of society. Even though the USA may not be a paradise on earth, even though its resources may not be as inexhaustible as some simple-minded Europeans used to imagine after the war, and even though it still has to face a number of grave problems – e.g. the race question and the rise in crime in the major centres of population – it is nevertheless essentially healthy and strong. However, in the long run, the USA will be able to honour its obligations only if it is not expected to do too much. The genius of the West, which is at work in the USA also, is beginning to evolve a new civilization that will usher in the post-industrial age. This civilization is now undergoing a change, a transformation of quantity into quality. But the Europeans will never see this promised land unless they succeed in meeting this challenge and responding to it. In other words, we have arrived at Europe's crossroads. We must show whether we can make the transition from the nation State to the continental State. Those who fail to make the grade will be of no account in the space age, whose dawn we are approaching; they will not even have a say in deciding their own fate. Jean-Jacques Servan-Schreiber was right in saying: 'Salvation must be the work of a political awakening.' And in a later passage he declares: 'This necessary transformation of Europe will not happen of its own accord. For this, we need politicians who are also men of resolution.'

After the two terrible civil wars which occurred in this century and which brought this continent from splendour to the very brink of an historic abyss within the space of one generation, it is the desire for the welfare State – occasionally also called 'social policy' – which has become the main motive power in Europe, while the determination to ensure Europe's political survival is on the wane. Europe's retreat from world affairs began with the surrender of the colonies, which could in any case not have been held indefinitely, and was to find its most tragic and striking symbol in the British withdrawal from the Far East, from east of Suez. But even this did not enable Europeans to find their happiness in some quiet corner and to maintain and cultivate their civilization in the shadow of the new constellation of World Powers. On the contrary, the great changes – political, sociological, scientific, technical, economic and industrial – the world has undergone, and the shifts in the balance and distribution of power bound up therewith, will deprive Europeans of the power to decide their own fate, i.e. the future shape of their civilization and even the issue of their external security. Even their right to be consulted in the making of these decisions will steadily be eroded.

Are Europeans prepared to make a stand and to take action against this trend? Are they ready to take the initiative? While it is true that a high standard of living can never be the main inspiration of political action, it requires political action to ensure such standards. Though some Europeans do realize this, rivalries and selfishness have prevented the necessary measures being taken. Europeans are wasting time, and time is of the essence. Some are aware of the facts but no longer have the will-power or strength necessary to do what is needed. They would rather see America dominate Europe than have Europe's resources amalgamated; this they consider a dubious, and even dangerous procedure, for a variety of reasons. Others believe that America has by now drawn so far ahead that there is in any case no chance of catching up with her. I am aware that American firms at present have long-term investments in Western Europe totalling 21,500 million dollars and that the aggregate investment abroad of US private enterprise rose between 1950 and 1966 from 17,400 million dollars to 75,000 million. I also know that of the foreign patents registered in the Federal Republic in 1967 more than forty per cent were American. But these things should not cause us to despair. We must not accept the view that Europe's only task is to serve as a domicile for American subsidiaries and a source of royalties for American patents, that her long-term defence is a matter for

American troops, and that, all in all, this is the most attractive future for Europe imaginable. People who think in this way do not realize that, assuming that this state of affairs continues, Europe will gradually lose the power to decide its own future and that this will happen even if Europeans do retain the formal attributes of sovereignty and self-determination. This will inevitably be so because the facts of the situation will simply prove too strong. Such people further overlook that total military dependence on the USA would mean that the ultimate questions of Europe's security would come to depend on America's not always predictable internal politics.

In this analysis there is common ground between the convictions de Gaulle expressed and my own views. However, I cannot go along with the General in his prescription for a cure. The General regretted Europe's lack of vision and determination in the face of the American challenge. He considered that France was the only laudable exception to this rule and that it was therefore up to him to act – or not to act, as the case may be – on behalf of Europe, even though he had received no mandate for this. He wanted to sacrifice nothing of France's sovereignty and of the distinct identity of the French nation; on the other hand, he was unable to persuade the other Europeans voluntarily to accept his political prescription for action vis-à-vis the USA. He therefore substituted France for Europe until such a time as the other Europeans mended their ways. This was his famous grand design with small means – his political do-it-yourself – which was a mixture of national awareness, vision of the future and resentment dating back to the last war. It is de Gaulle's undeniable merit that, after the breakdown of the integration plans of the fifties, for which he was not alone to blame, he called upon the Europeans to recover the vision of their historic mission and their sense of responsibility to themselves and warned them against blind dependence on the USA. He further warned that if Europeans do decide in favour of blind reliance upon the USA and cling to the latter's apron strings, a sense of 'over-commitment' is bound to arise in America. And this feeling was in fact reflected in the main question put by US Senators during their debate on the non-proliferation treaty. They wanted to know whether that treaty would result in the USA having to undertake even greater obligations towards its non-nuclear allies than is the case now. Furthermore, it is to the General's credit that he pointed the way to a new eastern policy, with the object of creating a sense of a universal European community.

However, we must make three reservations:

1. An individual approach by a European nation to Moscow, undertaken in an honest endeavour to promote European reconciliation and inspired by an awareness of one's own country's great culture and historic past, will not be rewarded by the Kremlin, which thinks in different terms. Moscow calculates in terms of actual and potential power and likes to play Europeans off against one another. Moscow does not take a divided Europe as seriously as she would a united Western Europe, a European Federal State.

2. If the other European States are to support France's ideas about an independent Europe, they must certainly not be expected to do so on the basis of a European isolationism directed against the USA. They will only support these ideas on the basis of a division of labour achieved with US support, which would restore to Europeans, step by step, the responsibility for their own security, give them a full share in American know-how – naturally on a basis of reciprocity – and which would make Europe the other pillar of NATO. The latter must be renewed so that it can remain in being after 1969, but it must be reformed and reorganized.

3. Let us assume that it were possible to persuade the political leaders of a number of West European States to adopt the French line – perhaps after the latter had been modified here and there. However, without common institutions of the federal type, institutions which member States would not be at liberty to abandon any more than California is free to leave the USA or Bavaria the Federal Republic, such a coalition, even if it were dignified with the name of 'confederation', would not last *à la longue*. In the event of a political change in a member country, with another coalition taking over the reins of government, sooner or later the policy of subordination to France would be relinquished. The confederal system can only remain during a transitional phase, which must not be too long. At the end of it, a federation must take over or else the old centrifugal forces will once more gain the upper hand behind a smokescreen of fine talk about Europe.

In his sensational book 'Formulae of Power' (1965), the nuclear physicist W. Fuchs declared: 'The figures show that in the course of the next two or three generations the European Powers will lose any significant influence among the nations which they may still possess unless they succeed in achieving genuine economic and political unity.' He declares – and he justifies his view by means of a series of diagrams – that a simple addition of national potentials cannot be a substitute for integration, since the latter pays extra dividends in terms of additional power. I, too, oppose a simple addition of national potentials because, in my view, such an approach must necessarily be futile inasmuch as it presupposes the taking of decisions by the unanimous vote of all States concerned – something that has hardly ever been achieved. Moreover, Fuchs may be wrong in his time scale, and in fact this process may be much more rapid than he thinks. Perhaps the 'point of no return' will be reached sooner – possibly as soon as 1980.

The OECD published a report in the autumn of 1967 which makes it frighteningly clear that the 'technological gap' which has opened up between Europe and America is rapidly growing wider. In this connection, it would be more correct to speak of a 'science and technology gap'. We may well ask ourselves whether our continent will not miss the bus, whether its industries can stay in the race if its countries do not decide, at long last, to spend more money on research and development and, in particular, if they do not co-operate more closely in this area and amalgamate their resources.

According to the OECD, the United States spent about six times as much on long-term technical and scientific projects in 1966 as the six members of the EEC and about three times as much as all the countries of Western Europe put together. Professor Karl E. Ettinger and Helmut Mylenbusch* report that the 700,000 researchers, technologists and engineers engaged on research and development projects in the USA in 1967 had a total of 24,000 million dollars at their disposal for the development of new ideas, inventions and products. A considerable part of this expenditure, they say, was borne by the US federal authorities and the remainder, some forty per cent, by private enterprise. And yet, the 'manpower potential' of the Old World, despite the brain drain to the USA, has not diminished as much as one might think. A

* 'Worldwide Enterprise', *Handelsblatt*, 2-3 August 1968

comparison between the numbers of American and EEC research workers and engineers shows that the proportion is of the order of 2.6 to 1; a comparison covering the entire Western part of our continent shows the proportion to be 3 to 2. In other words, Europe still has an adequate number of experts at her disposal, even though across the Atlantic their number is naturally higher. We thus still have a chance, but we have not much time to waste.

According to *Business Week\** 9,875 scientists and technicians entered the USA from abroad during the period 1946-66. Of this total, 3,612 came from Europe, and the implications of this for the future are clearly not too hopeful. According to a study by Dr Claus Müller-Daehn, the Federal Republic lost 1,780 scientists and 4,220 technologists to the USA during the years 1959-66. Currently, four hundred experts still emigrate from the Federal Republic each year, and more than two thirds of them to the USA. When one looks at the reasons, it becomes clear that it is not so much a matter of pay as of working conditions. In the USA, experts can go outside their university faculty and co-operate with industry as well as government establishments. Technical equipment is right up-to-date (even though there may be less emphasis on the creature comforts, so dear to our professors), and there is more freedom to move from job to job, less administrative work and more rapid promotion.

When one asks oneself just what the 'technological gap' is, one realizes that it would be by no means hopeless to try to close it if the European Powers were to join forces in a common effort. Professor A. P. Speiser, research director of the Brown Boveri Company, who used to work for IBM, is of the opinion that one can only decide whether a given continent has a decisive technical advantage over the rest of the world when one has made a systematic comparison between all types of goods produced – from spaceships to computers and from refrigerators to hypodermic syringes. As regards the USA, four categories of products can be distinguished on the basis of such a comparison.

1. In the following three categories the USA is greatly in advance of Europe: space technology, computers and aircraft construction.

2. Furthermore, the USA is markedly superior to Europe in

* 9 September 1967

the production of certain electronic components, especially integrated circuits, and in large-scale communication systems.

3. As regards the overwhelming majority of products, however, there is no marked difference. This applies, among other things, to the following areas of outstanding economic importance: motor vehicles, machine tools, domestic appliances, entertainment electronics (radio, television, record players, tape recorders), chemical and pharmaceutical products.

4. The USA is considerably behind Europe as regards railways, shipbuilding and watchmaking. In shipbuilding, however, both Europe and the USA have now been left far behind by Japan; the same applies to certain areas of entertainment electronics.

This, in rough outline, is the picture we get after taking stock of the situation. Are we justified in speaking of a one-sided technical advantage enjoyed by the USA? If it were not for the first category, we should be right to question this proposition. The Americans' enormous headstart in the fields of space technology as well as computer and aircraft construction shows, however, that they are advancing most rapidly in precisely those areas of technology which are decisive for the future. A few exceptions apart, one may say: the more rapid technical progress is in a given field, the greater is the USA's headstart in that field.

It is clear from what has just been said how marked technical and industrial progress has been in those areas which are connected with rearmament. This is an age-old – and none the less painful – truth. Even five hundred thousand years ago, when the light of reason first feebly dawned on man, giving him a presentiment rather than real knowledge, he invented a tool which he used both to make his day-to-day life easier and as a weapon with which to kill his own kind – the chipped stone. In the Upper Palaeolithic age, which began a hundred thousand years ago, the bow was developed as a weapon for use in hunting and war. It was the oldest device capable of performing a mechanical operation by means of stored energy. In classical times, people had sophisticated weapons for their campaigns and battles – catapults, siege engines and battle chariots. The siege and conquest of Tyre by Alexander the Great and the construction of a bridge across the Rhine by Julius Caesar are famous achievements of classical antiquity. It was war which gave rise to technology. In other words, to quote the definition given by Heraclitus in 500 BC, 'war is the father of all things' – or so it was in his day.

Archimedes of Syracuse, who lived in the third century BC, was one of the first genuine scientists to give a marked impetus to the art of warfare. A legend about him tells us that on his advice Roman ships threatening his country were set on fire and destroyed by means of mirrors reflecting the sunlight. He is also said to have claimed that if he were given a point to stand on outside the earth he would be able to lift our planet from its hinges – a hypothetical assumption which has become a palpable danger in our space age. Some hundred years before him, Aristotle founded the science of ballistics. Although he cannot be considered a scientist in the modern sense, since he blended his experimental findings with speculative theories which he postulated as being a priori valid, his theory of motion has been accepted without question for almost two thousand years.

After the invention of firearms – approximately at the turn of the thirteenth and fourteenth centuries – it became important to gain exact knowledge about the trajectory of projectiles. Niccolo Fontana, known as Tartaglia, devoted his researches to this problem. In 1537 he published his *Nova Scientia* and nine years later two volumes about the art of gunnery, with chapters about trajectories, the combustion of powder and the arts of aiming and making guns. He thus started the long line of scientists who devoted their lives to solving the practical problems of ballistics. This line stretches from Galileo Galilei in the sixteenth and seventeenth centuries – he was in the Venetian service as scientific advisor – via Isaac Newton in the seventeenth and eighteenth centuries and Adrien-Marie Le Gendre in the eighteenth and nineteenth centuries, up to Ernst Mach in the nineteenth and twentieth centuries.

The marriage between warfare and science, once concluded was never to be dissolved. It is, of course, a union of opposites, but despite the conflicts inherent in it, it has proved fruitful. One can draw consolation from history, which shows that the fusion of the two extremes of human endeavour – one the result of man's creative genius and the other that of his demoniac lust for destruction – has not always harmed, but has even on occasion, benefited the world. The enormous financial and intellectual efforts which have been and are being made to promote weapon research and development have yielded considerable economic dividends in the past and are doing so to this day. For the far-reaching demands which an army makes on its weapons and equipment in order to be sure that they remain, or become, superior to those of the potential enemy – or that they are at least not inferior to the latter's arms and equipment – have driven industry forward and impelled it to break fresh ground, advancing its skills further and further.

Arms technology has fostered and stimulated nearly all fields of industry. A great deal of 'spin-off' in the form of fresh knowledge has been gained in this way and has benefited the civilian economy. As examples one could mention the following: aluminium, the turbine, radar, bridge construction, the multi-fuel engine, sub-miniature technology, the use of ultra-high frequencies, electronics, the transistor, space travel and nuclear energy. All this goes to show how much our standard of living owes to military technology.

Despite the benefits which it has thus conferred on civilian life, modern military technology, which dates back to the end of the Middle Ages and the beginning of the Modern Age, has imposed heavy spiritual burdens on the scientists engaged in this field. The scruples which they feel to this day were expressed in a letter Tartaglia wrote to the Duke of Verona more than four hundred years ago:

It was at first my intention to write a treatise on the art of gunnery and to raise the latter to such a state of perfection as to make it possible to calculate the trajectory of every shot in all circumstances. . . . However, one day, as I reflected upon my actions, it seemed to me blameworthy, shameful and barbaric, and deserving of severe punishment by God and men, that anyone should dare perfect an art which does harm to one's neighbour and destroys the human soul and, above all, which causes Christians continually to make war upon one another. Consequently, I not only gave up these researches completely in order to be able to devote myself to other matters but tore up and burnt all my calculations and writings on these matters, full of remorse as I was at the thought of the time I have spent on this task. I firmly resolved never to commit to writing that which remained in my memory against my will, be it to do a favour to a friend or for self-interest, as I have often been asked to do. I came to look upon this science as a grave mistake, as the ship-wreck of the soul. Today, however, with a wild wolf ready to pounce on our flocks and with our shepherds eager to aid the cause of our common defence, it seems to me that it is no longer fitting to keep these things secret, and I have decided to make them public, partly in writing and partly by way of mouth, so that each one of us may the better be able either to attack the common foe or to defend himself against him. I now bitterly regret having earlier given up this work, for I am certain that, had I persevered in my efforts, I should have discovered matters of the utmost value – as I still hope to do in the future. . . .

Similar thoughts induced Albert Einstein to address in October 1939, on behalf of a number of physicists, a warning call to President Franklin Delano Roosevelt in the course of which he said that it had just come to seem that it might prove possible in the immediate future, to set off a chain reaction in a large quantity of uranium which would free immense amounts of energy and radium-like elements, and that this new development could lead to the manufacture of bombs. It was this fear which was in fact responsible for the production of the atom bomb that hit Hiroshima on 6 August 1945 and opened a new era of terror and uncertainty. It may be one of the ironies of history that it was a champion of peace who gave the starting signal for this development. Einstein addressed this warning to President Roosevelt, together with a call for the construction of an American atom bomb, out of fear that Hitler might make such a bomb before long. He went on to say that the fact that Germany had just halted the sale of uranium produced in occupied Czechoslovakia with so little loss of time was undoubtedly connected with the fact that the son of von Weizsäcker, German Under Secretary of State, was on the staff of the Kaiser Wilhelm Institute in Berlin, where certain American researches into uranium were being copied at the time. Just like Tartaglia before him, Albert Einstein was tortured by remorse and would dearly have liked to have undone that which he had done. His conscience impelled him to sign a memorandum shortly before his death – in April 1955 – which ended with his passionate plea to the statesmen of the world to the effect that since nuclear weapons were certain to be used in a future war and therefore constituted a threat to the continued existence of mankind, the governments of the world should publicly admit that a world war could not further their aims. He urged that peaceful means be sought to settle all matters under dispute.

A similar story is told by Max von Laue, who won the Nobel Prize for physics in 1914, of Otto Hahn, winner of the same prize for chemistry in 1946. Von Laue tells us that when Hahn – who was in a British internment camp at that time – heard that the first atomic bombs had been dropped on Japan, he thought of committing suicide because he felt that he shared in the guilt in view of his achievement in 1938 when he split the nucleus of a uranium atom. However, it should be noted that research was going on in this field at the same time in the USA and Britain, and I do not think I am detracting from Otto Hahn's achievement – in fact, I think this may help to exonerate him from any moral guilt – when I say that I am convinced that the atomic bomb would have been produced by the Americans during the second world war even if Hahn had not made his discovery.

Professor Stephen Possony, an American, has argued just as passionately – though in a different sense – in his book *The Strategy of Peace*, published in 1964. He took issue, violently and no doubt in somewhat exaggerated terms, with those who demonstrate in the streets to protest against nuclear weapons. He declared that mankind could only be 'liberated' from nuclear explosives if all scientists were first exterminated, and that in order to preserve mankind from the rediscovery of nuclear physics, a twentieth-century Herod would have to kill all newly born children gifted with an inventive spirit.

George Ball commented on this problem: 'Scientists ... did not create nuclear power; they simply disclosed it and made it available to mankind. Thus, if the world blows itself up, neither science nor the scientists will be to blame – only man's pathetic inability to order his affairs in a rational manner.'

If we look the facts in the face – however unpalatable they may be – we cannot but agree that America owes its rapid progress as the West's leading economic Power in large part to its efforts in the field of rearmament.

In 1975 about 40 per cent of the entire industrial output of the United States will be accounted for by products which do not as yet exist. Most of them will probably owe their existence, directly or indirectly, to research and development in the field of defence – of which, in the final analysis, space exploration and nuclear technology are but a part. Out of every dollar of their income, the

USA's aircraft and rocket builders invest 22.5 cents on such long-range projects. The corresponding figure for communications and electronics firms is 12.9 cents; for manufacturers of measuring instruments 11.8 cents, and for producers of electronic instruments 9.4 cents. Of the total of more than 20,000 million dollars which America spends, on an average, each year on such projects, about two thirds comes from the budget. Of these two thirds, in turn, 51 per cent is provided out of the defence budget; 28 per cent comes from NASA and 10 per cent from the Atomic Energy Commission. What rich dividends the capital thus invested is yielding is obvious from the fact that the results of US scientific and technological research and development are reported to double every seven years.

Since between them all the nations which live in the Western part of our continent devote only about one third the amount spent by the USA to research and development, it is easy to see why the gap goes on widening. According to French estimates, which in any case are several years out of date, the Federal Republic's annual expenditure on licences for foreign patents exceeds the revenue from this source by 600 million dollars. The figure for France is said to be 450 million dollars, and that for Italy 176 million dollars. It should, however, be noted in this context that the figure for Germany gives a slightly distorted and pessimistic picture. The fact is that German firms make the best of the provisions of the German-Swiss agreement on double taxation by ceding their inventions to their subsidiaries in Switzerland. The German parent companies pay royalties to their Swiss subsidiaries, which are registered as separate corporations. But even so, it must give us food for thought that, according to the monthly report of the German Federal Bank for July 1968, a sum of approximately DM768 million had been paid out during the previous year for foreign patents, inventions and processes. The report further said that during the last fifteen years the amount paid out in this way had grown at an annual rate of DM50 million. If things go on in this way at the current rate, in twenty years' time Europe will just about be able to manufacture indifferent copies of some of America's products. Wolfram von Raven has noted in this connection: 'It is hardly an exaggeration to say that a citizen of the Old World will feel almost as stupid in the twenty-first century when he meets an inhabitant of the New World as a Neanderthal man would feel were he to meet one of our contemporaries.'

True, we Germans are not alone to blame for the fact that such gloomy predictions are being made at the present time about the fate of our continent. The tendency of each nation to want to go it alone – which might well be called Europe's congenital disease – makes scientific and technical co-operation, which is required on a large scale, more difficult. An analysis of the main obstacles which stand in the way of better co-operation between German enterprises and firms in the five other EEC countries has been published by the German component of the European Society for Economic and Social Development (CEPES). It lists the following main difficulties: industrialists' inadequate knowledge of the possibilities of co-operation; differences in language and mentality; obstacles to the movement of goods across frontiers; differences in taxation and regulations on fair trading practices. Perhaps the efforts that have been made lately, e.g. by the Italians, to overcome these obstacles will prove successful. It goes without saying that the Federal Republic will have to do its share by submitting appropriate proposals and making money available for their realization. If this is to be done, it will be necessary, among other things, to carry out a structural reform of our defence budget. It will be our task during the next few years to make available the necessary means to finance projects, e.g. in electronics, which hold out the promise of economic benefits and which will, at the same time, further the cause of European unity. It should be possible to increase gradually the appropriations for research and development in military technology, which at present account for a mere five per cent of the defence budget, to ten per cent. We must bear in mind that partnership with us will be an attractive proposition only if we can offer something in return for what we hope to receive. In this connection, the Federal Republic, as well as the other countries of Europe, will have to face up to a problem which has been, and will continue to be, the subject of bitter political controversy – the share of public expenditure which investment and growth projects should be allowed to absorb. There can be no doubt that what we must do is quite literally to make a virtue of necessity and to restrict expenditure on other items in favour of such projects. This calls for the courage to adopt a set of priorities and to make political decisions regarding public expenditure which would reflect those priorities. It will be necessary to cut down on current consumption in order that we may safeguard our future. In the nature of things, a conflict arises in this connection between what is known as 'social policy' and 'political policy'. I do not wish to suggest, however, that I favour a reduction of all types of expenditure on current consumption. For example, money spent on fostering talent or retraining unskilled labour must be considered to come within the category of expenditure designed to safeguard the future.

I believe that it would be a step in the right direction if the proposals were accepted which were submitted by H. Neumann, professor at the Free University of Brussels and Chairman of the Société Nationale d'Investissement.* He called for a European Investment Corporation to be set up which would:

1. Promote the establishment, reorganization and expansion of European enterprises.

2. Support, or give an impulse to, industrial, commercial and financial projects serving the interests of Europe.

3. Foster technical progress and especially the industrial exploitation of the results of scientific research.

4. Promote, or encourage the launching of, projects based on advanced technology, as well as projects in the most progressive sectors of industry and in those regions of Europe which require development or reorganization.

5. Promote the establishment of enterprises of a joint or multi-national character.

If we Europeans agree to organize our budgeting in this sense and to co-operate closely we shall be able to learn much from the Americans as regards the management of research and development without necessarily copying them. We should also examine to what extent research and development can be promoted and foreign findings adopted directly for economic purposes without our first having to make the costly detour via arms expenditure.

The fact is worth noting that two thirds of all research and development work in the USA is being carried on, not by public institutions but by private enterprise. Nearly all the projects for

* *Handelsblatt*, 9 July 1968

which private enterprise is responsible – working, for the most part, of course, under State contract and with State finance – are being carried out by some two thousand firms. These activities are in the main concentrated in undertakings with more than five thousand employees, so that approximately eighty-three per cent of all the projects is in the hands of enterprises whose own annual research budgets exceed ten million dollars and which consequently have the necessary facilities for laboratory, development and testing operations. In Europe, industry's share in research and development is nothing like as great, and international mergers would be necessary to create enterprises of the required size. Moreover, the divisions which still beset our continent create obstacles so grave that they cannot be eliminated by co-operation alone.

Consequently, the following steps should be taken: We should standardize company and commercial law as well as the regulations governing the capital market in the European countries concerned; we should do away with taxation regulations that hinder international mergers and co-operation; a standard type of European company should be agreed by all the countries interested; finally, a set of standard European commercial, trade and capital market laws should be enacted. We must give up all wishful thinking that the Common Market – which still has to go through many stages (standardization of taxation, standardization of certain laws as described above) – can automatically develop into an effective political community. For such a community to be created, we need the vision and moral courage to take the necessary political decision. We must pool our resources and ensure that their use is immune from the veto of any of the Powers involved; we must have the courage to join hands in a common foreign and defence policy.

I would not wish to close this chapter about the 'technology gap' without quoting from an article published in the *Neue Zürcher Zeitung* in 1968 by Christian Lutz under the heading: 'The Technical Gap Between USA and Europe.' He says:

The USA's immense expenditure on research and development and its superior efficiency have had repercussions and spectacular successes throughout the world in space exploration, aviation and the most advanced branches of electronics. These are the roots from which the plant which we call the 'technology gap' has sprung – a plant which on closer examination turns out to be somewhat frail and which has, at all events, been rather ineptly named. Is Europe condemned to watch this gap grow wider? Will she have to rush breathlessly after her mighty competitor, whose tail light she can only just glimpse disappearing into the far distance? The very fact that we should ask these questions in itself underlines the danger inherent in this catchword about the 'technology gap'. It is that we attribute America's economic superiority to a single cause, whereas in reality this superiority is due to a whole complex of causes. Because of this misconception, efforts are being made to cure the trouble 'regardless of cost', as it were, through attempts to tackle the – supposedly single – root cause, while in reality any remedial action, to offer a prospect of success, would have to involve the use of all available means in the economically most effective way.

This, however, would necessitate an approach on a broader front, embracing educational reform on the national and European planes, national and European economic enterprise, old-type management as well as the management of the future. In turn, all these problems once again come down to the need for a political decision.

The political state of Europe is correctly described in the following frank analysis by George Ball:

To be sure, Europeans have taken the first step towards building an integrated economy – and that is a remarkable achievement – but they have made almost no progress toward the modernization of their political structure, so that today it is more archaic and creaky than it seems. Papered over by prosperity, internal divisions and instabilities lie just below the surface, weakening the political will and the capacity of national governments to make hard decisions, with the result that, while democracy survives, it does not flourish. . . .

Europe's political weakness has many causes. Not the least is the discovery by the European peoples that prosperity at home cannot be translated into power status on the world scene so long as it is achieved within political structures that are too small for present world requirements. The result is a disquieting paradox, since Europe's newfound sense of economic strength and well-being has been accompanied by the shrinking of political horizons.

Professor H. G. B. Casimir, a Dutchman who heads the research department of a world-renowned concern, defined Europe's needs in this ironic comment:

Let the US Federal Government be done away with; let the USA be divided into its constituent States and let steps be taken to ensure that each has its own separate taxation system, currency, banking and insurance laws as well as customs regulations. Let the American minorities be settled in as many separate linguistic areas as possible – fifteen at the very least – and let there be in each such area at least one competing minority language, necessitating the maintenance of a bilingual school system. And do not let us forget to introduce some forty or fifty different systems of patent regulations. When all this has been done, the technological gap between the United States and Europe will soon begin to shrink.

Thus, if we are to make progress, the first thing we must do is to ensure that Europe's resources are used jointly for major projects in the sphere of 'big science'. This will require a change of heart, the various nation States will have to give up asking short-sighted and greedy questions about whether they are likely to get their investments back in the shape of future orders and profits. If we fail in this then America's foreign-based industry will undoubtedly remain the world's third strongest industrial power and will go from strength to strength despite its current difficulties. Servan-Schreiber's thesis is entirely borne out by the facts given by Thomas J. Watson, Director-General of IBM, in October 1967. According to him, the goods and services supplied by foreign-based American firms total more than a hundred thousand million dollars, and these enterprises, taken together, thus rank third in the world as an economic power after the USA and the Soviet Union. He went on to say that in 1965 the seventy-five million workers employed in the EEC countries produced just under half the output turned out that year by the approximately equal number of US workers.

The remedy is not irrational anti-Americanism or a new mood of *laissez faire-laissez aller* resignation but the creation of a pro-European policy consisting of co-operation, fusion and integration in the right doses and applied pragmatically. In this connection, a few words ought to be said about the EEC, which is an essential – though not the only – instrument we must use to this end.

The EEC – which has always regarded itself as the most effective instrument for European unity – has from the outset of its efforts to promote integration been blamed for allegedly dividing Europe. Its critics fear that the EEC's economic regionalism will inevitably result in the disintegration of Europe, which is precisely the opposite of what is wanted. In view of the EEC's many joint policies in the most varied fields of the economy, the cry went up that there was a danger of discrimination against third countries, and a risk of undermining their trade relations with the members of the EEC. I believe that during the few years that have elapsed since its foundation, the EEC has in fact furnished adequate proof that these fears are groundless. Admittedly, the fusion of several national economies into a single economic area is not taking place in static conditions. The unavoidable structural changes in the economic situation cannot be confined to the countries directly involved in this fusion but must affect, to a greater or lesser degree, the economies of third countries, according to the extent of their involvement with the member countries of the EEC.

But to say this is not to condemn the EEC; to do so would be to overlook the true facts and aims of its members. The truth is that the Community has developed into a growing international market. Since its establishment, the EEC has succeeded in almost doubling its aggregate imports from third countries as well as its exports to them. If you bear in mind that the Community depends on its own ability to export if it is to maintain and even increase its social product and that it lacks the necessary energy and raw material resources to meet its own requirements at low cost, you are bound to agree that this situation cannot be a mere coincidence. There is no question here of any inward-looking discrimination or desire to create blocs. The same outlook is also reflected in the aims of the Community's member countries. These aims do not provide for a Little Europe and a Greater Europe as alternatives to choose from but assume that the former is merely a preliminary stage leading up to a great united Europe. The German Federal Government, in particular, has always stressed that the Community's character as an open organization must be reaffirmed again and again. This applies both to the external trade of the EEC with third European countries and to the establishment of closer links between those countries and the EEC.

It came as no surprise, therefore, that the actual results of the establishment of closer ties between the Six gave the lie to the fears of the Community's critics, inasmuch as this process has actually stimulated moves in favour of integration in countries which do not belong to the Community. Several of these countries have come to see in the EEC not only an attractive trading partner but an organization offering a useful base for closer co-operation between the European States. However, the EEC must not be compared to a company in which one can buy a share by investing capital, nor a club which merely expects its members to show a spirit of fellowship. The Community is an organization which has grown up as a result of the joint endeavour of all its members and which must place great demands on those who wish to join it, both in its own interests and in those of Europe as a whole. The fact that the Community is an open organization must therefore not be understood as meaning that the right of entry is automatic. The EEC expects both its present members and any countries which wish to join it in the future to satisfy stringent criteria. In this connection, it seems essential that newly joining States should be expected to accept the Treaty in its present form, including all its general objectives and all the decisions adopted to date.

If you think that you can 'have your cake and eat it' you will get nowhere – and this also applies to the cause of European unity. However you look at it, a price has to be paid by the European Powers in terms of diminished sovereignty for the sake of our continent's future.

# 10 *Security for Europe*

I remember all too well an experience I had during my first few weeks in office as German Minister of Defence. It was the time of the Hungarian rising and the Suez crisis. Chancellor Adenauer was on a visit to Paris that evening, when Bulganin announced that the Soviet Union would destroy Paris and London with nuclear rockets if Britain and France did not put an end to the Suez operation and withdraw their troops from Egypt. The Federal Chancellor and the French Premier happened to be dining when the news reached them. They agreed that the French Ambassador in Washington should sound out the State Department to see if the Americans were ready to react to this threat forthwith. At that time, the American presidential election campaign was in full swing and occupied the whole of President Eisenhower's attention. Secretary of State Dulles, a man for whom we had, and, still have, great admiration, could not be reached. Only Assistant Secretary Herbert Hoover was available in the State Department, and he did not feel able to give Hervé Alphand, the French Ambassador, a satisfactory reply. Asked whether the United States would react with a threat of massive retaliation or not, he gave a non-committal answer.

My own personal view was then and remains to this day that the Americans would in fact have reacted at that time because they simply would have had no alternative. I also believe that the Soviet threat was largely bluff. But the fact that M. Alphand was forced to cable back an unsatisfactory reply was, I am convinced, the real reason for de Gaulle's subsequent decision to speed up the development of the French nuclear arm and to proclaim France's total national independence in this area. There were two reasons, apart from those usually mentioned, why the French decided to speed up and intensify this work. One was their belief that the possession of atomic weapons and the ability to use them as they saw fit would give French policy a more solid base. Secondly, they were convinced that once France had such a weapon in her own hands, this would remove the last particle of doubt about the Americans, unconditional willingness to expose themselves to the risks of a nuclear war for the sake of Europe's freedom. Admittedly, this argument cuts both ways.

I do not wish to be unfair to the Americans, but the problem is not whether a sceptical attitude towards them is justified or not – the fact is that it exists. By frequently changing their strategic doctrines, and also as a result of certain statements made by prominent leaders, the Americans have themselves contributed to this uncertainty. We have had the Radford doctrine, then the John Foster Dulles doctrine, which was a modified version of the former. We have witnessed the introduction of atomic weapons into the alliance. The allies received nuclear weapon carriers, with the actual weapons remaining under American control. Then we had the McNamara doctrine, with its variants ranging from the 'counter-city strategy' to the 'counter-force strategy' (the latter providing for action against military targets only). Later still came the theories of 'crisis planning', 'escalation' and the pause which would intervene in a future war after a conventional phase and before the atomic nuclear threshold was crossed. Finally, there came the views of US disarmament delegate William Foster, which have been haunting the couloirs ever since. According to an article which he contributed to the review *Foreign Affairs*, the West must be prepared to accept an 'erosion of the alliance' as the price to be paid if a non-proliferation treaty is to be agreed in bilateral negotiation with the Russians.

I have already commented on the current strategy of the so-called 'flexible response'. It betrays signs of a 'Vietnamization' of the NATO concept, i.e. of a tendency to follow a doctrine of 'controlled warfare'. As a result, it is open to question whether, in the event of a conventional attack on Europe, the Americans would make available the nuclear weapons which they have stationed here for use by local forces, and it is even more doubtful if they would use their own strategic weapons. But the fact of the matter is that the conditions for a conventional defensive war are in any case completely lacking in Europe, regardless of the extent to which the military forces over here are integrated. In other words, if the United States were prepared, in principle, to have its methods of warfare in Europe dictated to it by an aggressor from the East, the latter might conclude that the risks he would have to run in a war were easily predictable; at all events, such an aggressor might assume that the West's military strength was inferior. That this should be so is due, in no small measure, to the fact that the level of military forces available in Europe for immediate action has been and still is developing, thanks to the military planning of the Europeans themselves and to the partial withdrawal of the Americans, in a direction diametrically opposed to the postulates of official theory.

It would be wrong, however, to blame the American Government for openly embracing the strategy of limited defence, for it is bound to consider the security of its own continent and the preservation of its own population to be its primary responsibility.

For the first time in its history, the USA is exposed to the danger of devastation in the event of war. It knows that the Soviet Union is already in a position to destroy simultaneously a minimum of two hundred targets in America, killing between fifty and a hundred million people in the process. It is inevitable, and indeed only natural, that this knowledge should cause the Americans to modify their attitude to the problems of European defence. The Americans do not by any means wish to avoid their share of the responsibility for the defence of the free peoples of Europe, but they are looking for ways of ensuring that the defence of Europe, necessary though it is, does not automatically expose their country to sudden destruction. In the missile age, the Soviet Union and America confront each other much more directly than ever before, and this confrontation has caused Europe to become, geographically speaking, a peripheral area.

The peculiar character of American military power tends to be much more widely misunderstood on the continent than, for example, in Britain. The United States has taken over the essential role of Anglo-Saxon sea power, but on a new and vaster scale which also embraces the air and space. As a continent in its own right, situated between two oceans, America has all the typical characteristics of an island. To wage war on foreign soil, America needs an expeditionary corps, and this can only be sent into action if she has command of the lines of communication by sea and air. The military consequences which result for the United States from this geo-strategic situation cannot conceivably be consistent with European requirements. The dilemma which bedevils the joint strategy of NATO – something which to all intents no longer exists – stems from this very fact. The United States is involved at all points of the globe: across the waters of the Arctic it faces the USSR in a direct military confrontation by rocket, and a similar confrontation has also resulted from the operations of Soviet nuclear submarines in the Pacific and the Atlantic. On its Western flank, the USA, notably Hawaii and the other US forward bases, face the new Asian World Power, China. To the south, the United States is certain to become increasingly involved within its own hemisphere – politically, economically and possibly also militarily.

It is therefore simply unrealistic to call the United States a European State'. However much individual Americans may feel that their roots and traditional links tie them to Europe, geography and a different way of life have created a specific complex of interests for America – which has become a large island and cannot escape the fate of a great island Power. But the spiritual and ideological bonds which exist between Europe and America can nevertheless be invaluable to mankind's future. The Atlantic partnership – a partnership between the nations which together make up the advanced civilization of the West, the nations linked to one another by the Atlantic – the Mediterranean of the modern age – is probably the most valuable concept to have emerged during this century. It is up to us to preserve this concept intact and to make it a living fact. But if we remain stationary too long at the first stage of this Atlantic evolution, the stage reflected in the outmoded concept of NATO as established in 1949 and in the treaty providing for American protection for Europe, we shall endanger the future of the free world. We Europeans have a responsibility for our own destiny which we must allow no one to take from us. In this connection, the question of our own defence must not be viewed in isolation, since it cannot be separated from the problems and facts of our economic and political viability. By their passive attitude, Europeans have been guilty of violating the letter and spirit of the NATO Treaty. Article 3 of that document calls upon the signatories to strengthen the alliance by effective self-aid and mutual support. This aspect of the matter became of great importance to Europeans when the position of the United States vis-à-vis the Soviet Union began to change as a result of the atomic stalemate; the confrontation with a Red China which was steadily becoming more powerful; and the US involvement in its own hemisphere. Europe should have concentrated all its energies on perfecting the independent defence of its territory as soon as these developments became evident. Such action is now urgent, nor is it unrealistic to expect this effort of Europe.

The great countries of Western Europe have the necessary human, financial and economic potential to build up their common defence in a joint endeavour. Their only military and strategic handicap is their lack of space. Western Europe cannot afford to allow, in its military planning, for extensive retreats to be followed by successful counter-attacks. We lack the necessary 'operational depth' for this. It is this very fact which forces Europe to adopt a specific defensive concept of its own, a concept which is simply unthinkable without an independent deterrent.

In 1967, a number of events occurred in the world which showed us how important it is that we Europeans should take the initiative of our own accord because, failing this, we shall increasingly over-extend the resources of our transatlantic ally.

The first of these events was the war in the Middle East. 'A little fire is quickly trodden out, which, being suffered, rivers cannot quench.' The wisdom of William Shakespeare's words was to be confirmed once again in this war. The drama which took place in the Middle East in 1967, and which has not yet ended in a mutually acceptable settlement, is likely to have repercussions on world affairs which will be at least as grave as those of the 1962 Cuban affair. The duel, fought mainly in the Sinai Desert, not only changed the position at the actual scene of the encounter but demonstrated to the world at large that the situation of 'atomic stalemate' between the Great Powers is producing effects which are different from anything envisaged heretofore. The small Powers have had to realize that guarantees of protection and aid, regardless of the form in which they are given, cannot be relied upon absolutely. They are liable to prove of doubtful value 'when the chips are down'.

A review of the course of events to date shows that the Israelis inflicted an initial political defeat on the Russians with their lightning military victory over the Arabs. The Israeli success at first upset Russian calculations. The Soviets first became interested in the Middle Eastern crisis because they felt they might be able to turn it to their own advantage. This is why they filled the arsenals of the Egyptians, the Syrians and the Iraqis with vast amounts of up-to-date military equipment. The outcome of the war which resulted from this – although it must not be assumed that the Russians definitely wanted it to break out – thwarted their intentions since it ended in a setback for them. Moscow was compelled to disappoint Cairo when the latter asked for direct assistance in the hour of its defeat. The weakening of Russia's position in the Eastern Mediterranean which resulted from this was, however, only apparent.

In the second act of the tragedy, the Kremlin actually succeeded in considerably strengthening its position along the southern shores of the Mediterranean – once regarded by the West as its *mare nostrum*. Precisely because he came out second best, Gamal Abdul Nasser is more dependent on the USSR than ever before. Russia's purpose in re-equipping him with an abundant armoury of weapons of aggression was to get him to make available to her, by way of payment, bases for the Soviet Navy and Air Force. The Russians, profiting from Arab hostility to the Israelis, have penetrated into the Mediterranean with their Navy. Already the conventional fire power of the Soviet Navy in the Mediterranean – even discounting the nuclear support it may possibly receive from air bases on the Egyptian mainland – exceeds that of the combined British, French and Italian fleets in the Mediterranean.

Scarcely less important is the fact that the United States showed itself incapable of 'crisis management' when the decision between war and peace rested on a knife's edge. The ambitious Egyptian leader drove off U Thant's blue helmets by simply clapping his hands as one would scare away a flock of birds from a newly sown field, and then began to blockade the Gulf of Aqaba. Finally, he forced King Hussein of Jordan into an alliance with him. All this in practice amounted to an Arab attack on Israel – and when it happened the attitude of the USA was one of hesitation. It was afraid to take the aggressor to task and in effect did nothing to prevent the outbreak of hostilities. As soon as the first shot was fired Washington proclaimed its neutrality 'in word, deed and thought'.

What was it that paralysed America at the moment when everybody expected her to act? No doubt, the USA's readiness to act was affected by the thought that it would become involved in a direct confrontation with the USSR if it attempted, by means of a demonstration of its military might, to put an end to the blockade of the Straits of Tiran. Washington was, moreover, undoubtedly hoping to settle the conflict in co-operation with Moscow 'in a spirit of relaxation', which would probably have been impossible without prejudicing the interests of Tel Aviv. Considerations of domestic policy also unquestionably influenced the attitude of the White House, especially the fear that too great a burden might be placed on the nation if it were drawn into yet another involvement, in addition to the Vietnam war.

A review of the facts thus leads one to the following conclusion: the powder keg in the Middle East blew up because it had been crammed full of explosives by the USSR. As for the USA, it was unable to put out the smouldering fuse. Let this be a warning and a lesson to us! Since one cannot rely absolutely on Russia's intentions, the American 'peace preservation strategy' does not function with automatic certainty. It presupposes, in addition to the necessary material resources, a psychological readiness on Washington's part to use the deterrent. As we have now clearly seen, this cannot be depended upon in all circumstances and at all times. As for Europe, divided as it was and therefore too weak, it played no part whatever in these events although they took place on its doorstep.

The other development we Europeans should regard as a lesson is the Vietnam war. I believe that Lothar Ruehl was right when he said:*

The idea that America is certain to defend Europe in all circumstances, even in the absence of an adequate European effort, is false. Clearly, this notion has now in any case been shaken. Europe can trust America only so long as the European nations show themselves more worthy of

* *Die Welt*, 4 April 1967

trust and confidence than South Vietnam. Europe cannot afford to trust America blindly and cannot leave the burden and responsibility of protecting its nations exclusively to whoever happens to be President of the USA.

The end of the American involvement in Vietnam is not yet in sight. But after the Vietnam war nothing will be the same in the Atlantic alliance. It is conceivable that America will then be prepared to show more interest in Europe and to make more of her resources and energies available to her than in the years that went before. But this is by no means certain. The European allies have not made it easy for the American super-power to carry the burden of the Vietnam war. The warnings given by de Gaulle, to the effect that the United States should not allow itself to be drawn into a war which it could not win at an acceptable cost but in which it might well lose its prestige as a Power and an ally, have proved justified. It is therefore possible that America will decide to stand further aloof from Europe in future, politically and militarily, than hitherto. The psychological result of America's Asian experiences may be that she will come to think in terms of her own continent.

Many Europeans have failed to realize that American protection for Europe has never been absolute but has always borne a calculated relation to the risks, costs and results in prospect. Whatever the outcome of the war, the course of American policy in Vietnam shows the value of the lesson which American statesmen from Truman, Marshall and Acheson right up to Eisenhower, Dulles and Kennedy – i.e. the statesmen who were in office at the time of the alliance's greatest era – have again and again tried to impress upon Europeans, to wit that nothing in this world can be had free of charge and that America can and will only help those who are prepared to help themselves.

What developments should we expect in the course of the next decade? I believe that the following French prediction is substantially correct – or is at least not false:

1. The worldwide rivalry between the United States and the Soviet Union, reflected in their arms race, will negatively affect the 'balance of terror'.

2. The cohesion of the two power blocs will be further weakened because each of the two leading Powers faces difficulties at home and abroad in maintaining its position. France's position within one alliance has its parallel in that of Rumania in the other.

3. A further element of uncertainty stems from the fact that the future role of the Chinese People's Republic, as well as the course

of events in Asia, Africa, the Middle East and Latin America, are as yet quite uncertain.

4. The proliferation of nuclear weapons may be slowed down but cannot be prevented altogether since it is likely that nuclear technology will make progress everywhere. This remains true in spite of the non-proliferation treaty.

5. In Europe, where the situation appears to be relatively stable in spite of the German problem, there will be a risk of certain conflicts of interest, 'frozen' by tacit agreement, flaring anew.

One can only agree with this analysis, as well as with its conclusion that the crises which we must expect to break out in many parts of the world may grow into conflicts and subsequently into major wars. There is no reason to deny the logic of its warning that France, without being directly involved in the first place, may eventually be drawn into such conflicts because one or the other of the protagonists may wish to seize her territory and its resources or to prevent the other side from so doing.

How does France propose to cope with the turn of events she foresees, both in military and defence policy terms?

Under President de Gaulle Paris clearly intended to supplement its strategic nuclear potential, which was thought adequate to provide a continental-scale deterrent, with weapons capable of being employed for intercontinental deterrence.\* De Gaulle worked towards an objective he outlined in a speech at the St Cyr Military Academy as long ago as 8 November 1959: 'Since France is liable to be destroyed from any part of the globe, her armed forces must be able to go into action in any part of the world.'

The bold scheme to create a system of nuclear defence effective at all points of the compass, which it was apparently planned to complete by 1980, has had a sceptical reception in Germany and has even met with criticism and opposition here. Nevertheless, no one doubted that the self-willed man on the Seine would carry out his intention, defying all opposition. However, his programme was delayed by the shock of the May–June 1968 strike and its economic consequences. The former Minister of the Armed Forces,

---

\*At the time of writing it is unclear how France's post de Gaulle policy will turn out, though there have been hints of the intention to maintain a nuclear strike force and of the desire to share nuclear know-how with the USA and Britain. – Tr.

M. Pierre Messmer, was probably right – from a purely French point of view – when he stated* that no one was able to offer an alternative to this programme. In politics, he added, only that can safely be destroyed which can be replaced by something else. France must in fact further expand and improve her *force de dissuasion* – as she has been calling her *force de frappe* for some time – if she is to prevent it becoming a museum piece during the course of the next ten years.

The dispositions which Paris has made for its future defence policy are therefore quite sound in theory, though this does not answer the question of whether these plans are in fact feasible. Did President de Gaulle not overrate the economic and financial resources of the nation in assuming that it could afford the armoury of a World Power? It is not enough to have rockets with a range of six thousand miles or more; such missiles must be equipped with devices which will enable them to pierce an enemy defence system. Moreover, they cannot be fired at random; there must be exact advance knowledge of the prospective targets. A complicated apparatus is thus necessary, the precise cost of which cannot be estimated in advance.

On the other hand, it would be a mistake to regard de Gaulle as having been fanatical or uncertain of purpose, a man who chased blindly after utopian visions without calculating precisely the real possibilities of a given situation. Admittedly, his plans may not have given due weight to fiscal considerations. He probably based his action on a political speculation running somewhat as follows: America's nuclear presence in Europe will gradually dwindle to zero. This will sooner or later compel the continental countries to shelter under France's protective umbrella. In return, they will not only recognize France as the leading Power but will pay hard cash for her protection. And who would be bold enough to say – in view of all the neo-isolationist tendencies in the USA – that this calculation was wholly unrealistic?

The General's 'inimitable style' – as it has aptly been called by Professor Henry A. Kissinger – with which he was wont to introduce and execute his plans, should not blind us to the fact that he pursued France's national interests, which he equated with those of Europe, with cold logic.

*Revue de la Défense Nationale, March 1967

At this point we should examine the role of Britain, who originally acquired a nuclear capability of her own, both in order to underline her global role and as a means of 'reinsurance' in view of her insular position. What is the importance of this nuclear potential today, now that the situation is changing?

It seems to me that London is trying to underline its membership of the nuclear club not only by advocating, with a zeal which nearly equals that of Moscow and Washington, that no further members should be admitted, but is also seeking to demonstrate, by developing its own nuclear potential, that Britain is one of the Great Powers. Her first nuclear submarine, armed with sixteen Polaris missiles, is now in service, having successfully completed her firing trials off Cape Kennedy. The Minister of Defence, Denis Healey, lost no time in giving public assurance that the vessel is, of course, at NATO's disposal. However, we must not take this too literally since Britain naturally has not the slightest intention of ceding the power to issue orders for the use of her nuclear arms to the alliance. This she regards as her own preserve. In other words, her attitude differs in no way from that of France.

At the moment, London can still claim to be one rung above Paris in the hierarchy of atomic Powers. By the end of this decade, the British will have three more 'underwater cruisers' in service in addition to Resolution – Repulse, Renown and Revenge. Her nuclear fleet will then be equipped with a grand total of 64 missiles of 128 megatons of TNT – the equivalent of 6,400 Hiroshima-type bombs. This considerably exceeds the capacity which the French are likely to have at their disposal at that time. Britain thus remains the largest of the small Powers since she continues to rank – though she is vastly inferior to – immediately below the United States and the Soviet Union among the possessors of nuclear arms, with France and China following Britain in the table.

However, this situation could change quickly, since it is becoming increasingly clear that London is unable to keep pace with technical progress. Britain does not want to replace the Polaris missiles installed in her submarines with missiles of the Poseidon type, which are more modern. This means that she is deliberately renouncing the possession of weapons capable of breaking through a hostile defence system. She has also had to cancel the purchase of fifty US F-111 bombers, which means that she is giving up the 'airborne component' of her nuclear armoury. Paris, on the other hand, has no intention of limiting its plans in the same way. Unlike the British, the French are allowing for a 'broad spectrum' of land and sea-borne missiles, as well as manned bombers, in their programme. One may thus conclude that the French intend to remain capable of action as an atomic Power while Britain is willy nilly abandoning the struggle.

The day of decision in this strange arms race, which these two European Powers have been engaged in for ten years now while the two giants remain locked in their nuclear stalemate, thus seems to be drawing closer. Since Britain, who at first thought, thanks to her 'special relationship' with the USA, that she could afford to take things easy, is gradually running out of steam, it would seem that France, who had to rely on her own resources from the outset, may hope for a 'victory'. But whether Paris will in fact be able to reach the position in world affairs which it is striving for and to keep it for any length of time, even if it should succeed in going one better than London, is doubtful.

In the end, the nuclear competition between the French and the British, which in the last resort is a competition for the leadership of our continent, may turn out to have been not only pointless but positively harmful. For the Anglo-French controversy, which also affects other areas, such as the EEC, is an obstacle to the unity of our continent. It follows that the interests of the Old World as a whole would be better served if Paris and London would agree to co-operate in their nuclear policies instead of competing.

Some British circles have in the meantime come to realize that it was a mistake to reject the offer de Gaulle made in 1962 to Macmillan, the then British Prime Minister, to the effect that British and French nuclear arms development should be pooled. One can now hear opinions voiced in London that Britain would have been able to 'buy' her way into the EEC through nuclear co-operation had she grasped this opportunity. Perhaps it is still not too late for this, provided the British revise their Nassau Agreement, under the terms of which they acquired their Polaris submarine missiles, thus underlining their 'special relationship' with the USA. Washington would be well advised to encourage the British to pool their nuclear rearmament efforts with those of France with a view to thus creating the kernel of a European nuclear Power. And, in general, Washington would do well, in its own interests, to prepare the Europeans for the day when they will have to carry the main burden of responsibility for their own security within the framework of a future NATO.

It would certainly be difficult for Paris to turn down such a British offer, especially if America were to announce at the same time that she was prepared to agree to a reform of the alliance on the basis of a European-American partnership. Washington could add to the practical effect of such an approach by announcing that it was prepared to make US technical know-how available for a joint Anglo-French nuclear rearmament programme. There can be no doubt that if this were done ways and means would be found of effectively preventing a further spread of nuclear arms without discriminating against other great countries. The Federal Republic and, I believe, Italy, too, would not feel that they had been treated unfairly in regard to nuclear defence provided a beginning were made with the creation of a European nuclear armed force in the shape of an Anglo-French atomic armoury, in the expansion and development of which they could participate in appropriate ways.

In June 1967, by which time the nuclear problem had already become topical within the alliance, President Kennedy asked me: 'What would you do in my place?' He did not really want my advice; it was just his way of testing other people's views. Kennedy may have expected me to criticize France's *force de frappe*. However, I explained to him that he would be best advised to try to achieve a satisfactory understanding with the French regarding an American contribution to their nuclear rearmament. France, I said, would never be prepared to accept a position in the nuclear field inferior to that of Britain. She would always strive for nuclear parity with Britain notwithstanding the repercussions this might have on her relations with the USA. If America rejected such a policy, she would sooner or later find it virtually impossible to keep up the pretence of friendly relations with Paris.

I then said to the President that as the Soviet potential grew so did the risks facing America. In making his decisions, he was bound to be exposed to growing Soviet pressure as a result of the nuclear stalemate. So long as he alone in the Western alliance had nuclear arms at his disposal, the Soviets would be in a position to threaten his country directly should he decide to give nuclear aid to Denmark, Germany, Italy, Greece or Turkey. The situation would be different if the American President were in a position to say to the Soviets: 'I am all for peace, but unfortunately you have attacked one of our allies. Up to now, America's arms have not been in action, but if these attacks do not cease, they will be.' Such a flexible American strategy, which would not entail the use of American power from the outset of a conflict, will only be possible, however, when Europe is able to defend herself. But failing this, that strategy would expose our continent to the danger of a conventional war – and thus to an increased risk of armed conflict – since an aggressor would then no longer be faced with unpredictable dangers.

Events since this conversation took place have confirmed me in my belief in the correctness of my opinions. True, the obstacles to European unity have become greater, but they are not insurmountable.

The real reasons why the EEC has been going through a difficult time and why it has proved impossible to convene a ministerial conference about a political union of the Six are, in my view, as follows. Under de Gaulle France concluded that her partners were not, in actual fact, prepared to join in a common defence policy; her partners, on the other hand, suspected France of wishing to impose her hegemony on them, of harbouring anti-American sentiments and wanting to 'go it alone' with Moscow. Anyway there has been no lack of hints from the French during the last years under de Gaulle that Paris might be prepared to contribute its nuclear power to a European organization once Europe's political unity had been achieved. We should make a start here by at last taking up the ideas about a European Defence Community outlined by de Gaulle in his Strasbourg speech. I admit that the French President was inconsistent inasmuch as he stressed that these days the security of a State could only be safeguarded if it had sovereign control over a nuclear armoury, while at the same time he refused to accord this privilege to the other Great Powers of Western Europe and blocked the path to an integrated Europe endowed with its own sovereignty. I surely need not repeat here that, for fundamental reasons, we have no wish to acquire national control over nuclear arms for the Federal Republic. However, neither do we wish to exchange our mighty protector, America, for a French nuclear patron, the less so since the latter's nuclear potential is very weak. What we want is a substantial common European effort.

The 'strategic solidarity of Europe', of which de Gaulle so often spoke, could in my view be organized along roughly these lines:

1. The creation of a European Defence Community, which should and must be established as the 'second centre of the alliance', must be preceded by the setting up of a European political community. The latter must define its attitude to the following problems: East-West relations; strategic doctrine; control of atomic weapons; relations with the 'Third World'.

2. Such a community cannot be established, however, through immediate integration, since the peoples of the Old World are not yet ready to see their identity submerged in a 'Federal Union'. It must therefore take the form of a union of States which would be represented by a joint body consisting of Ministers delegated by the various governments concerned.

3. The permanent political executive of the community should consist, at the very least, of representatives of the six Common Market countries, without, however, excluding the possibility of British accession. Eventually, a directing body might be formed in the shape of a consortium consisting of delegates representing France, Italy, the Federal Republic, Britain, plus one other member country (the latter alternating). This body would be advised by a team of independent experts.

4. Below this executive (and expressly subordinated to it) would be joint staffs for the operational command of the armed forces, as well as authorities in charge of co-ordinating European arms production and logistics. There would also be a joint office for operational research. Military planning for the defence of the continent would follow clear political directives and co-operation with the United States in defence policy would consequently proceed on a basis of partnership.

5. Military nuclear planning would be the task – after a European atomic strategy had been defined by the political executive – of special commands consisting of representatives of the two European nuclear Powers (France and Britain). These commands would have the further task of ensuring co-operation with America's

nuclear arm and keeping the non-nuclear Powers – which would have full voting rights in the political executive – informed of the details of any decisions reached.

I do not wish to give the impression that this is a cut-and-dried 'plan'; it is a 'model' which allows of many variants.

Only by making constructive suggestions aimed at achieving a genuine increase in Europe's influence and at stabilizing conditions within the Atlantic community can we overcome the present dangerous stagnation of Western policy. We shall not succeed in this so long as we go on sweeping the real problems under the carpet. If we wish to ensure that Europe is in a position to exert an influence of her own on the future destinies of the world, without our vital links with the USA being thereby affected, we must be prepared to adopt a bold policy based neither on total dependence on Washington nor dictated by fear of France's aspirations to a position of hegemony.

But has not another path been long since taken which will lead us a long way from the ideal of a European Defence Community?

'We must have a European peace system' is the political slogan which is all the rage nowadays. But should you ask the people who indulge in such talk just what exactly they mean by this phrase, you will get nothing definite out of them. All you will be told is that the alliances, both of the West and the East, must give way to a 'system of collective security', which could be something like a regional UN. All the nations of our continent would have to undertake not to use force against one another and to punish by collective action any State which had violated this undertaking. As a result, all the countries of our continent, large and small alike, would be confined within their national frontiers, prevented from forming alliances and from thus guaranteeing one another's continuing existence.

The Soviet Union, whose pleas for such a solution are the loudest, has received much applause for this – and not in the East alone. One may in fact well ask onself to what extent the USSR's 'partners' really agree with it. But at all events the Soviet Union has been receiving increasing support in the West for its proposals, which at first sight seem quite reasonable. But we should do well to take a closer look at what lies behind this programme. It is not as difficult as it might seem to glimpse, under the cloak of the

'European Peace System' with which the Kremlin has now draped its figure, the cloven hoof of naked power politics. The USSR is not even trying particularly hard to hide its real aims. In fact, it has made its intentions clear beyond any doubt by defining its demands in detail.

A 'system of collective security' – so Moscow keeps telling us – must, of course, include the Soviet Union. The United States, on the other hand, need not necessarily be a part of it, since the USSR belongs to Europe and the USA does not. If the Americans insist on having a say in the Old World, the Russians could do likewise in the New World, and this Washington does not want. Therefore Europeans can and must deal with their own problems without outside interference. The Kremlin considers it to be a condition for the establishment of a 'peace system' in our continent that the White House should proclaim its indifference to events over here and should, as a visible token, as it were, bring its troops home from this side of the Atlantic. We are thus dealing with a new version of the old slogan: 'Yanks Go Home!'

There is no denying that the Soviet Union, unlike the United States, is a European country. However, this is only part of the truth. Firstly, because two thirds of the USSR's territory is in Asia, and secondly because as a Super-Power the Soviet Union considerably outranks all the other Powers of our continent. A Europe which had turned its back on America would therefore be bound to be dominated by Russia. Those who have learnt the lesson of history must know that any 'peace system' worthy of the name must be based on a balance of power. And who would seriously wish to spread the *pax Sovietica*, which holds sway over the Eastern half of our continent, to the Western half, where the *pax Americana* has to date been ruling supreme? Even if the USSR were prepared to accept the USA as a partner in furnishing a joint guarantee, it would be certain to insist on a withdrawal of US troops and the dissolution of NATO. In other words, Europe would then have a guarantee which would have to be implemented at long distance. In the midst of all these speculations, we must not overlook that the USSR has in recent years greatly increased its military strength in all fields, successfully pursued its quest after nuclear parity with the USA and never given up its strategic objective of achieving the neutralization of Europe.

In its present state, the free part of Europe will only be able to preserve a measure of autonomy provided it can retain America's protective cover, even if the latter is increasingly thinned down. A change in this respect can occur only if our continent unites politically, i.e. if a new Power arises which will make it unnecessary to import military strength from across the Atlantic. It would be reasonable to expect those who believe that the USSR is worried by the American presence in Europe to look to Moscow for support for the creation of a European Power. But it is precisely this which the Kremlin opposes, thus proving that its propaganda for a 'system of collective security' is merely a vehicle for its bid to expand its sphere of influence – and who would be prepared to countenance any such thing?

We Europeans shall achieve an acceptable peace system only if we succeed, by our efforts on behalf of West European unity, in gradually persuading the USSR that there is no better solution from its own point of view than a really fair settlement which would offer security both to the Soviet Union and to our continent as a whole.

# *11*  *Mastering the Future*

Germany is the geographic centre of the new European constellation which I have just described. Her political evolution, coupled with the successful rebuilding of her economic potential and, above all, the latent desire of all Germans for reunification and a more stable and comprehensive European structure will play an essential part in the events to come.

This will be decisive for our future course of action since, in a way, it determines our tasks. Politics is the art of the possible or, to be more exact, it is the skill of a group, a community, a State in asserting its own interests as best it can in the face of contrary trends while, at the same time, creating a community of interest with the maximum number of political partners. No matter how complex and varied the interests of our State, free Germany, may be, in the last resort – even though officially we may sometimes be told a different story – these interests have always been subordinated to three vital obligations which we must honour:

1. We must preserve and consolidate, against all dangers from within and without, the freedom of our State, a freedom which history has vouchsafed us yet again – and after the events of the recent past I regard this as a divine grace.

2. We are called upon to restore in peace the freedom of the whole of Germany, and this can only be done provided Europe as a whole is free.

3. We must grasp the need to forge the unity of free Europe, our larger fatherland, in order that a strong pillar may thus be built to support the bridge linking the Old and the New World.

These three demands, which derive from our interests, are

160

interdependent. If we are to safeguard the security of the Federal Republic, we must strive to create lasting foundations for co-operation between the peoples of our continent and its American daughter, and only if the freedom of our country has been safe-guarded, can there be any hope of reunification within an all-European framework. Similarly, it is only our partnership with other nations which can give us hope that one day this reunification will indeed be achieved in the form we desire.

This should give us an idea of the significance of 'interdepend-ence', of the interweaving of interests which must decide our view of the situation. What determines our scope of action? Since politics is primarily a matter of power, it is the extent of our power which defines and limits the possibilities open to us. In this con-nection, we must not think that the power of a State is determined exclusively by its possession of military resources and its ability to use them. This is all the more true in this atomic age, since war can no longer serve as a 'continuation of politics by other means', as defined by Clausewitz. An armed conflict would presumably extinguish our nation's physical existence, and we must thus not only refrain from looking for trouble but must try to prevent a conflict by all means at our disposal. However, should an aggressor put our existence in mortal peril, we should have to accept the challenge.

The scope of our military power as a usable instrument is thus limited. Nevertheless, our armed forces remain of considerable importance, for they determine our value as an ally. This, in turn, will decide whether, and to what extent, our partners will be prepared to take account of our interests. 'The day is past,' George Ball rightly points out, 'when a nation like Germany, with a population a third as large and a national income (allowing for inflation) only a quarter as great, could – even for a brief time – dominate Europe and threaten the world. For the quantitative requirements of world power have increased three- or four-fold in twenty years. . . .'

But our economic potential, too, gives us power. In world trade, it has allowed us to move up to second place. It goes without saying that the use of that potential for political ends in a free community is possible to a very limited extent only, since, as we know, economic life tends to go its own way in pursuit of profits, regardless of politics. Profits create prosperity, which, in its turn, is essential if there is to be social security.

In gauging the power at our disposal, we must, further consider our legal and, finally, our moral position. Precisely because the world, aghast at what was done in Germany's name during the years 1933–45, still regards us with distrust, we must make certain – and we must do so with even greater care than both our partners and our adversaries – that our political efforts accord both with objective ethical norms and with the requirements of the law. This also means, I need hardly stress, that we must always resist demands upon us to renounce, for the sake of real or apparent advantages, our well-founded rights.

To sum up: the extent of our possibilities is determined by the extent of our power. The latter, in its turn, depends on a series of factors: the degree to which we are essential, in military terms, to our partners; our economic power; and our moral and legal position. Naturally, the right use of these factors is not a matter of arithmetical skill – it calls for the art of statesmanship.

We have seen that our vital interests are decisively determined by foreign affairs, and this has been true of our country throughout the ages. This is so largely because our frontiers are open on all sides; not one of them 'defends itself', as it were. Our thinking must therefore in the first place be determined by foreign policy considerations. This is obvious in regard to our defence policy and natural in regard to our European policy, but it is also a matter of course where our German policy* is concerned. Though the latter relates to our own country, it must not be seen as part of our domestic affairs and least of all must it be viewed in isolation from all our other problems because, as I have pointed out, our German policy is closely and indeed inseparably intertwined with these problems which concern, or ought to, concern us. Although it is true that our domestic affairs do have a bearing on our German policy, in the final analysis this aspect is of secondary importance, despite the fact that it is sometimes pushed into the foreground and given pride of place in a certain propaganda which is trying to manipulate the public's emotions in an effort to create illusions about a relaxation of tension. Among our people, this aspect of the

*I.e. the German Federal Republic's relations with Eastern Germany – .

matter is receiving a dangerous degree of attention, almost to the exclusion of everything else.

We have thus seen that our vital interests depend on one another; we have further seen that we are concerned here with problems of foreign policy. Our attitude to these problems and our efforts to solve them must therefore be subject to the 'interdependent' worldwide interests of our partners and opponents.

It will have become evident from the foregoing analysis that I give pride of place to our European policy, because our success or failure in this respect must, in the last resort, determine our fate both in regard to our security and to our national problem. We must concentrate such means as we possess on our efforts to promote the unity of our continent; this is the only way we can conceivably master the future. What other alternative is there open to us, especially since we are rightly being pressed to master our past?

Many people believe that a single thread runs through the history of this country. This thesis begins, to put it briefly, with the false allegation that Germany must be held responsible for the first world war; it then speaks of Germany's undeniable guilt for the second world war and ends with the accusation that Germany is now preparing a third world war. Bismarck, Wilhelm II, Hitler and Adenauer are said to have succeeded each other in direct line and are associated with one another. This theory is being assiduously nourished by the Soviet propaganda machine and has been taken up in various forms by many countries. Thus, there are authors and historians who try to justify the division of Germany on the alleged grounds that it offers the only chance of preventing a third world war. This propaganda is very effective, and many arguments are being adduced to support it. But Germany would cease being a source of doubt and fear once the 'German problem' had been 'Europeanized' and German affairs merged in a greater European organization and unit.

I have no illusions about the dangers inherent in the 'German problem', which is beginning to get on the nerves not only of our Western neighbours and allies but also of the neutrals. We must destroy the legend, widespread in many Western countries, that Germany has an inborn lust for aggression. The existence of a nationalist party is said to be proof of this theory. On the other hand, it is encouraging to see not only that these views are being countered by our friends in the West (often in the form of rather feeble lip service), but also that the peoples of Eastern Europe, e.g. Czechoslovakia and Rumania, are giving less and less support to this Soviet propaganda.

David Ben Gurion, the grand old man of Israel, declared in New York in the spring of 1967 that he does not believe in the danger of a rebirth of Nazism in Germany. He went on to say that he considered Kurt Georg Kiesinger's government to be in every sense democratic and that, in judging a country, it was the principles by which its government determined its action that mattered, while the views of a splinter party, such as the NPD in the Federal Republic, were of little importance. Extremist groups, he added, could also be found in the United States and Britain, without anyone making a fuss about it.

We owe a debt of gratitude for his generous plea on our behalf to this noble politician who represents the Jewish people. These were the words of a real humanist eager to plead the cause of justice, who has therefore repeatedly urged that the sons should not be punished for the sins of their fathers. These were the words, too, of sober, statesmanlike wisdom, of knowledge and experience, the words of a man who has learned from history that it benefits no one when a nation is condemned for all eternity to play the role of villain in the world. These were the words of a man who perhaps understands our problems better than we do ourselves. These were the words of the man, who, in April 1967, addressing the same Chancellor in Bonn, declared almost prophetically that the unity of Europe – i.e. a United States of Europe – must be created as rapidly as possible and that this must be regarded as a priority task. Only thus, he went on, could peace be safeguarded and a third world war avoided. For to create Europe, he declared, means to safeguard peace – and he was speaking on the eve of the Middle East war, in which we were to see starkly exposed the immobility of the Americans, the impotence of the Europeans and the power aspirations of the Russians.

When the Israelis had won an impressive victory within a few days, following the principle of 'God helps those who help themselves; – it's no use waiting for the others', and occupied territories which they are not prepared to evacuate unless their continued existence is safeguarded by a formal, guaranteed peace, they were accused by the Soviet propaganda machine of being militarists and using Nazi methods – an example of how cynically these catchwords are used by the Soviets.

A dangerous sense of inferiority has long since taken root in our minds. Our understandable desire to overcome the past has given rise to a morbid anxiety to view our present exclusively from that angle. Moreover, partly through autosuggestion and partly because people have for so long been trying to convince us of this, we are beginning to imagine that we are the world's outstanding political simpletons and scapegoats. We are thus gradually becoming obsessed with a sense of our own inferiority, and this has repeatedly prevented us from putting our case as forcibly as others are in the habit of doing.

Cramp is usually the result of excessive effort. We were to see this demonstrated strikingly in the 1967–8 discussions about the non-proliferation treaty. Having first been afraid to register our objections to our Anglo-Saxon allies' plans calmly and in time, we then sprang into action hectically, one might almost say explosively, at the eleventh hour. As a result, there was a risk of our exposing weak spots to our opponents.

We acted like a child which, after first being afraid to walk through a dark room, then starts singing in the dark so loudly, to allay its own fear, that the neighbours begin to complain.

Because we do not want to be unpopular and are anxious not to arouse false suspicions, we are hesitant about taking political action at the right time and in the right way in order to influence the course of events. Owing to our hesitation we become involved in situations where we are forced to react to accomplished facts that can no longer be changed. As a result, our statements – especially since they are made with a guilty conscience – often take on a violent and hysterical tone. Having first allowed ourselves to be carried away by the boldness which we have at long last managed to summon up, we lose heart just as quickly when we see – or merely imagine that we can see – that it is no use persevering. Afterwards, all is hangover and bitterness.

Psychologists call this 'frustration'. By this they mean the feeling of an individual or a people that it is no use trying to do anything.

165

Some of our 'intellectuals' are doing their utmost to spread a mood which is bound to make this disease worse. What they are saying is, to all intents, that we should confine ourselves in our political efforts to being 'good boys'. As a result, the impression has got about abroad that, however defiantly we might act at times, in the end we always come to heel. In turn, this enables our demagogues at home to spread hostility among the German people towards their neighbours.

Having learned wisdom from the parables and visions of the Old Testament and the experience of his own community, David Ben Gurion is aware of the risks and consequences inherent in this train of events. His views are prompted by concern for the future. While urging our American allies to show understanding for us, he is at the same time calling on us – without expressly saying so – to recover our self-confidence. Though we must be careful to adopt a modest tone in view of the moral debts we have incurred, this must not prevent us from pursuing a policy which gives due weight to our own needs.

Two points must be distinguished. Full recognition of the past mistakes and crimes of German policy, and a balanced, sober and sensible political attitude towards Germany's present and future tasks. The past cannot be overcome without a clear idea of what needs to be done in the years to come. One aspect of this must be our endeavour to make 'historical reparation'. Germany has played a fateful part in helping to bring about the collapse of the old European family of States. What better way could there be of making reparation than by now contributing to the rebuilding of that selfsame European family? We must play a major part in bringing about Europe's unity and overcome our past by renouncing all national sovereign rights. We shall thus help to establish a new Europe and promote the progress and development of the entire continent.

Like other people, the German people do not wish to go through another war. They are also eager to have a stable government based on the rule of law and to promote social justice in their country. The German people therefore want to be able to look forward to a secure future in a peaceful Europe in liberty and in solidarity with their neighbours. All this is based on the hope that the past will not be allowed for ever to stand in the way of the future and that sooner or later it will prove possible to wipe the years 1933–45 off the slate. The Germans do not wish to carry the burden of the past for ever. They do not want to be isolated or discriminated against because there has been a Hitler, because there have been concentration and extermination camps. Above all, they want their next generation to grow up in a normal atmosphere. In other words, they wish that generation to be burdened neither with national megalomania nor complexes carried over from the past.

What are the obstacles?

According to George Ball:

The doctrine of original sin has no place in world politics, and those who would erect it into something structural and permanent are themselves guilty of a sin against experience and common sense. A new generation is rising in Germany that will not willingly accept special restraints. Sooner or later the new Germans will react against inequality or discrimination; for no people so proud and competent will play the sedulous hostage to history and we would be stupid indeed if we thought otherwise.

While foreigners widely regard the Germans as a capable and dynamic nation, they consider them politically unpredictable and inscrutable. Consequently, the Germans are thought to constitute a potential risk. The greater and the more powerful Germany grows, they believe, the more important becomes the unpredictable element in the situation and the greater the danger. What can we Germans do about this? We cannot give up our dynamism; we cannot destroy our industries; we cannot change our geographical position, nor can we force our population to emigrate. What we can do is to co-operate in the construction of a European edifice as members of a European community which can absorb the German problem and as members of which the Germans will become 'predictable' because it will have become impossible for them to be anything else. This is the historic task which our generation must solve in order to reconcile the world to the German problem and all the memories it entails.

The free world needs Germany's co-operation for its own protection for the defence of its freedom àgainst the totalitarian threat from Right and Left. The problem is not how to ensure that

Germany, while strong economically, remains weak politically and impotent militarily – this would be to approach matters the wrong way. The real problem is how to add to her economic strength and political influence. This, far from being a threat to the world, would be of advantage to it. In the long run, a Germany which is an economic giant but a political dwarf is unthinkable. This is why German politics needs a European framework. As George Ball has noted, the forward march to a politically united Europe gives the new German generation a chance of playing a more constructive part, with self-respect, within a framework wide enough to give full scope to its talents. This is the only way the Germans can achieve full equality of rights with the other Europeans without frightening anyone – and fear is just as harmful to him who creates it as to him who has to suffer it.

At this point I am reminded of the principle formulated by Federal Chancellor Adenauer: We do not want to wait until the next generation, which is not burdened with the sins of the past, has taken over power. We should profit from the experience, suffering and hopes of Germany's middle generation. These are the people of my own age, who bear the scars of Hitler's disastrous policies. The overwhelming majority of my generation is not burdened with any past involvement in politics, but since we had to live through that time, we may perhaps be able to discern the demands of the future better than the next generation.

Throughout Europe, in our own country no less than elsewhere, it seems to be above all the young intellectuals who are in revolt against the 'establishment', which in their opinion does not know how to move with the times, considers its self-perpetuation to be an end in itself and has no aim beyond this. We should look upon this unrest, this criticism which young people are directing at us, their elders, as a call to action and a warning that we have not yet fulfilled our task.

According to the findings of a public opinion poll issued in May 1967, 78 per cent of West Germany's population would vote in favour of a United States of Europe if they were given the chance. Among young people aged from 16 to 29, and also among the intermediate generation from 30 to 44, the vote in favour would be as high as 82 per cent. It is particularly striking that of those who passed their university entrance examination, no fewer than

94 per cent want a United Europe. A strenuous effort aimed at achieving the unity of our continent would thus have a big majority in its favour, and I believe that the same is true of the other peoples of our continent. This is still the case today, but things may change if the years are allowed to go by without action. We must not disappoint these hopes – which represent an untapped pool of energy – but must try to live up to them by our actions. 'If hope for a United Europe is throttled, and the "Western orientation" continues to appear as a dead end,' says George Ball, 'a new German generation may well feel compelled to reverse the thrust of German policy.'

The destiny of our old world will be determined by the answers to the following five questions:

1. Do the nations of Europe, after the defeats which they have inflicted upon themselves in the two greatest wars of this century, retain sufficient confidence in themselves?

2. Do they have the courage to tackle the second technological revolution with their own resources and by exchanging information with others – a revolution which was triggered off by the creative minds of Europe but which has so far been carried forward on a continental scale exclusively by the Super-Powers?

3. Are they prepared to accept an appropriate share of responsibility for their own security?

4. Are they prepared to assert their right of self-determination by taking a share in the processes of decision-making on a world scale?

5. Will they show sufficient determination to assert themselves as a community of peoples capable of existence and action in the face of the steadily growing might and superior competitive strength of the Great Powers, or will they, in a spirit of national selfishness, go on trying to preserve their illusions about their separate identity as States, i.e. will they seek their happiness in some quiet corner, which in fact no longer exists on this earth?

We must act for the sake of Europe's youth. What we want for them is not the adventure of war, such as the last two generations have experienced, but the adventure of the future, for which they must be prepared, particularly in view of the fact that human history is proceeding at an ever increasing pace. We must conquer a new dimension, which will be the future living space of all the

European nations. We must create a way of thinking and a new awareness which will help us to grasp that we shall be able to remain Frenchmen, Germans, Italians, Britons or members of any other nation only if we genuinely become Europeans, and if we do so in good time – *urgentibus imperii fatis*, as Tacitus would say – under the menacing pressure of destiny.

# Postscript

More than half a year has elapsed since the publication of the German edition of my book and I therefore think it useful to bring my account up to date. Much that appeared unclear to many as recently as last autumn has now emerged with almost frightening clarity. If Europeans do not grasp before long that they must find a common response, equal to the historic occasion, to the challenge with which they are confronted, Europe will finally miss what chance it has of being allowed to embark upon the future as a more or less independent unit.

Self-deception was bound to end in disappointment. At the beginning of 1968, thinking in the Federal Republic and elsewhere – in complete accord with opinion and moods within NATO – was dominated by the notion that the West was well on the way towards an understanding with the East. It is to be hoped that twelve months later there are not many people left who do not realize that the models of a 'peace system' which certain people had so zealously constructed following various blueprints of a 'system of collective security' are unrealistic in present conditions and that these conditions will not change of their own accord. Those of us who keep their eyes wide open and are prepared to ignore the slogans which have been put forward, slogans whose authors misinterpret the situation either deliberately or out of credulity – those, I say, who are prepared to look the brutal facts in the face will have to prepare themselves for the following developments which may occur in the course of the next few years.

1. Relations between Washington and Moscow, far from being based on co-operative coexistence, are more likely to be fraught with the seeds of future conflict. It is therefore well-nigh inevitable

that any arrangements the two giants may conclude in regard to the technology of rearmament will be at the expense of our own continent.

2. Our continent – split as it is into two camps – has long since ceased to be able to shape world events and has degenerated into a passive object of those events. It is no use counting on a liberalization of political institutions in Europe's communist half, let alone on a restoration of the traditional system of nation States from the 'Atlantic to the Urals'.

3. On the contrary, Europe should be on guard lest its democratic half be forced – in the absence of the necessary measure of willingness and ability to achieve unity – to exchange the present Pax Americana for a Pax Sovietica – i.e. a state of affairs in which the free nations would have to accept compliance with Russian wishes as a *conditio sine qua non* of their existence.

Despite the attempts of certain people to repair the torn veil of error, illusion and hypocrisy with which they had sought to conceal the true facts, the Kremlin's strategic policy is clearly discernible. During the night of 21 August 1968 the Soviets consolidated the *cordon Stalinaire* which surrounds their European sphere of influence by occupying Czechoslovakia. By so doing they showed up as utterly false the thesis that they might conceivably be prepared to loosen their stranglehold on their empire and to allow it to change into a 'commonwealth' of sovereign nations. The military occupation was later supplemented with a political doctrine proclaimed *ex cathedra* – though certainly not invented – by Leonid Brezhnev. According to this doctrine, the Soviet Union claims the right to intervene in any State of the communist camp which is held to have gone too far in adapting its internal institutions and external contacts to its own interests. At the same time the USSR is bent on intimidating by means of brutal threats any 'capitalist' country which is not willing to accept this state of affairs. This was reflected in the announcement that the Soviet Union might wish to have recourse, as a stick with which to beat Bonn, to the UN Charter's clause regarding the status of 'former enemy States'. In return for not invoking this clause – a step the USSR sees as an enormous concession, in accordance with the slogan 'I'll give you an apple if you give me an orchard' – it expects to have its most far-reaching wishes met.

If one absolutely insists on bending over backwards, one might just allow that this may only be a hysterical exaggeration of a basically defensive policy. However, the offensive nature of Moscow's activities can be clearly discerned from the following two facts:

1. The Soviet Union has long since abandoned its former naval strategy of coastal defence in depth, a strategy which was well suited to its security requirements as a continental country and, instead, has made its appearance on the oceans of the world as a naval Power. It has advanced on both the sea flanks of Europe – chiefly in the Mediterranean but also in the Atlantic – in order to reinforce the pressure it is exerting on the 'mainland centre' of our continent through a pincer movement. If you think this analysis is a product of the old cold war mentality or a piece of inveterate anti-communism, then you must denounce the usually much-praised and admired Tito as an incorrigible warmonger. For, during the last few months, Tito has made enormous – and costly – efforts to turn his country into a fortress dotted with countless small strongpoints favoured by the terrain. In other words, Tito has rearmed both morally and materially.

2. It is clear from Soviet nuclear strategy that the USSR is bent on amassing a larger stock of intercontinental ballistic missiles than the USA. It is endeavouring – e.g. by developing orbital weapons – to alter the 'nuclear stalemate' situation in its own favour. The USSR's existing superiority in intermediate missiles thus acquires a new – and threatening – meaning for Europe.

Is it to be expected, in view of this situation, which will cause them to make considerable efforts to bolster their own security, that the Americans will be willing and ready to give additional guarantees for Europe's security for an unlimited period? Nor should we underestimate the fact that Richard Nixon – although he probably attaches more importance to the alliance with Europe than to any arrangement he might be able to arrive at with the adversary – is faced with problems, not only in regard to rearmament but also in other fields, the solution of which will demand much effort and money. Can we afford to believe in the miracle of Europe's continued ability to live on given, borrowed or leased American resources? After all, we have seen the US Senate oppose most strenuously, during the debate on the non-proliferation

173

treaty, the idea of America's furnishing additional security guarantees in return for the signature of her allies, 'freed' from the need to maintain a nuclear armoury and condemned to military impotence.

Europe needs power resources of its own to safeguard its freedom. It does not by any means want these resources with a view to using force against outsiders; it wants them to avert the use of force by outsiders against itself, and it wants to achieve this aim not by war but in peace. Power is thus not to be confused with force; rather is it an instrument designed to overcome force in the service of a policy aimed at safeguarding the legal order of society, at promoting its cultural and economic progress without prejudice to the interests of others, and at fostering the prosperity of the people. The concept of 'power', moreover, is not purely military in character; in fact, it covers a broad spectrum of multifarious factors, both measurable and imponderable, constant and variable. These factors lie between two extremes: the power of ideas, aimed at persuasion, and the power of armed force, aimed at vanquishing resistance. In itself, power is neither good nor evil; it becomes good or evil by the ends for which it is used and the way and extent to which it is applied.

Those who agree, and say so, that Europe must respond to the challenge with which it is faced contradict themselves if, in the same breath, they advocate that Europe should renounce the possession of power. Such people are daydreaming about the world they would like to see and fail to see the world as it is. The historic events through which we have lived, to our cost – and through which we are continuing to live second by second as the hands of the clock move on – have made it clear to us that to enforce right you need power, for otherwise power will mock right. It has been Germany's fate, through her own fault, that she has had to learn this lesson. It is not to satisfy an irrational ambition, nor in order to assert her national aspirations on a larger scale, but because she has good reason to be concerned about her own and her neighbours' continued ability to enjoy the privileges of autonomy that Germany is pressing for a sovereign Europe in which she would submerge her own sovereignty, the continued viability of which has now become questionable.

The facts – even those, and perhaps particularly those, which appear in the debit column of German history – however regrettable and contemptible they may be, in no way detract from the correctness of this prognosis and postulate for the future. One cannot help feeling, however, that Moscow – conveniently disregarding the sanguinary chapters in its own history – will continue its efforts to 'master Germany's past' until it is too late for Europe's future. And there are many 'useful simpletons' about who are helping Moscow in this.

*Franz Josef Strauss, February 1969*

## Acknowledgements

The following copyright sources are drawn upon in this book in quotations that appear on the pages cited:

George Wildman Ball, *The Discipline of Power. Essentials of a Modern World Structure*, Boston and London, 1968 (pages 12, 45–6, 98, 110–11, 115, 118, 133, 138 and 167); Winston S. Churchill, *The Sinews of Peace*, London, 1948 (page 21); Ernst Jünger, *Der Weltstaat. Organismus und Organisation*, Stuttgart, 1960 (page 34); Wilhelm Cornides, 'American Thinking on Security and the Peace Policy of the Free World' in Donald G. Brennan, *Arms Control, Disarmament and National Security*, New York, Toronto and London, 1961 (German edition *Strategie der Abrüstung*, Gütersloh, 1962) (pages 40–1); André Beaufre, *Introduction à la Stratégie*, Paris, 1963 (page 42); *Frankfurter Allgemeine Zeitung*, 3 May 1967 (page 50); *Neue Zürcher Zeitung*, 16 August 1964 (pages 65–6 and 137–8); *Die Welt*, 4 April 1967 (pages 148–9).